101 Ways to Prepare Soups & Salads

By

Aroona Reejhsinghani

PUSTAK MAHAL®

Publishers
Pustak Mahal®

J-3/16 , Daryaganj, New Delhi-110002
☎ 23276539, 23272783, 23272784 • *Fax:* 011-23260518
E-mail: info@pustakmahal.com • *Website:* www.pustakmahal.com

Sales Centre

- 10-B, Netaji Subhash Marg, Daryaganj, New Delhi-110002
☎ 23268292, 23268293, 23279900 • *Fax:* 011-23280567
E-mail: rapidexdelhi@indiatimes.com
- **Hind Pustak Bhawan**
6686, Khari Baoli, Delhi-110006
☎ 23944314, 23911979

Branches

Bengaluru: ☎ 080-22234025 • *Telefax:* 080-22240209
E-mail: pustak@airtelmail.in • pustak@sancharnet.in
Mumbai: ☎ 022-22010941, 022-22053387
E-mail: rapidex@bom5.vsnl.net.in
Patna: ☎ 0612-3294193 • *Telefax:* 0612-2302719
E-mail: rapidexptn@rediffmail.com
Hyderabad: *Telefax:* 040-24737290
E-mail: pustakmahalhyd@yahoo.co.in

ISBN 978-81-223-0017-0

Edition: 2011

Printed at : **Param Offsetters, Okhla, New Delhi-110020**

Contents

INTRODUCTION

A bowl of steaming hot soup makes a very warm and comforting drink especially during rainy season and cold winter months. But, otherwise also, throughout the year, warm soup is a very delicious food for its appetizing, stimulating and nutritious qualities. And, when taken with a bowl of salad, it becomes a complete meal in itself. Salads have come to be accepted as an integral part of the usual lunch or dinner. Salad stimulates the appetite and gives a high degree of satisfaction through eye-appeal, flavour and texture. The palatability of a salad mostly depends upon the type of vegetables which are used in its preparation. When making a salad, the most important thing to keep in mind is to use only fresh, tender and crisp vegetables. Always remember that salads are very much of your own making. With a bit of imagination, you can churn out eye-catching salads. This book contains recipes not only for simple crisp, cool and light salads for daily consumption but also for elaborate ones for the enjoyment of the whole family.

Aroona Reejhsinghani
502 B, Lila Apartments
Opp. Gulmohar Gardens
Yari Road, Versova,
Mumbai- 61
Ph. 6360224

Garnishes for Soups

Chicken or Mutton Soup: Sprinkle on one full grated egg yolk combined with sliced parsley or coriander leaves. Garnish with a cube of butter and rings of lime.

Vegetable Soup: Sprinkle grated cheese. Put bread courtons here and there and in the centre a big dollop of cream.

Minestrone Soup: Garnish with grated cheese, sliced parsley and bread courtons. Or, you can even mix in 3 tablespoons each of cream and butter and sprinkle on top grated cheese and parsley.

Corn or Tomato Soup: Garnish with cream flowers and vermicelli fried to a nice golden colour. Put whipped cream in a pastry bag and cut it into fancy shapes on a waxed paper. Freeze till the mixture becomes firm, and then put into the soup.

Basic Soups

Basic Soups are known as stocks, like chicken stock, mutton stock or vegetable stock.
There are two types of basic soups or stocks: vegetarian and non-vegetarian.

Non-vegetarian Stock is made from bones, meat scraps or other waste parts of meat and poultry. To prepare this stock, wash the bones and meat scraps and soak them in water for half an hour. Then cook for one hour in the pressure cooker to get the extract from meat and bones. Cool and strain through a cloth and use it.

Vegetarian Stock is made either from tomatoes, or from mixed vegetables.

Tomato Stock Take 1 kilo tomatoes, 1 bay leaf 3 cloves. 1 inch piece of ginger, minced. 1 small onion, minced. Salt to taste.

Boil tomatoes in 5 cups water with all the above ingredients. Remove the spices and strain through a sieve. Use this stock as per your requirement.

Vegetable Stock Take 250 grams mixed vegetables like cabbage, radish, carrot, celery, onion and turnips. Boil in 1 litre water till it is reduced to half litre of liquid. Strain through a sieve and use as required.

You can store these stocks for a few days in the fridge. In place of vegetable stocks, you can also use the water in which you have boiled your vegetables.

AROUND THE WORLD WITH SOUPS

HUNGARIAN GHOULASH SOUP

Ingredients (Serves 6 to 8)

- 250 grams each of cubed mutton, pork and beef
- 100 grams Ham
- 3 medium onions, chopped
- 2 big tomatoes, diced
- 4 green chillies, minced
- 2 medium potatoes, peeled and cubed
- 1 tblsp. chilli powder
- 4 sausages, cut into 1-inch pieces and fried
- Salt and pepper to taste

Preparation

Heat 1 cup oil and fry onions and chillies till soft. Add mutton, pork, beef and ham and fry till golden. Add tomatoes and 10 cups boiling water and cook till the mutton is almost done. Then add potatoes and spices and cook till both the mutton and potatoes are done. Add sausages to the soup and serve hot.

Irish Potato Soup

Ingredients (Serves 5)

- 6 medium potatoes, peeled and diced
- 1/2 cup each of milk and cream
- 1 carrot, sliced
- 2 medium onion, sliced
- 1 bay leaf, 1 clove
- Salt and pepper to taste

Preparation

Put potatoes, onions, carrot in a pan along with 10 cups of water and spices. Heat the contents When the vegetables turn soft, remove the pan from stove and cool. Strain the mixture through a sieve. Add milk and cream and reheat before serving. You can sprinkle grated cheese and chopped parsley on top.

Italian Fresh Greens Soup

Ingredients (Serves 8)

- 1 large head lettuce chopped
- 2 cups assorted green leaves of spinach, chawli and bathua sag
- 2 stalks of celery, diced
- 10 cups mutton or chicken stock
- Fried bread croutons, grated cheese
- Salt and pepper to taste.

Preparation

Mix together greens, onions, seasonings and stock, and cook till the greens are done. Remove from heat, cool and strain through a sieve. Reheat and add 3 tblsps butter. Serve hot with bread croutons (bread cubes) and cheese.

Italian Minestrone Soup

Ingredients (Serves 6)

- 1/2 cup each of boiled boneless chicken and mutton
- 100 grams noodles cooked according to the directions on the noodles pack
- 1 cup grated cheese
- 250 grams mixed cubed vegetables like carrots, potatoes, cucumber, peas, french beans and cabbage
- 2 tblsps flour, 1/2 cup milk
- 2 cups tomato juice
- Salt and pepper to taste

Preparation

Mix flour in milk. Mix vegetables, with chicken stock and tomato juice and cook till tender. Add mutton, noodles and chicken. Add milk gradually while stirring all the time. Mix in 3/4 tbs. of the cheese and sprinkle remaining cheese on top. You can make vegetarian minestrone by omitting meats and using water instead of stock.

South American Cream Cheese Soup

Ingredients (Serves 6)

- 2 medium onions, minced
- 2 flakes of garlic
- 3 tblsps. Tomato ketchup
- 1/2 cup each of peas and corn kernels
- 2 big potatoes, peeled and cubed
- 250 grams cream cheese mashed to a paste
- 2 cups milk, 2 eggs
- 25 prawns, cleaned.
- Salt and chilli powder to taste

Preparation

Heat 4 tblsps. oil and fry onion and garlic to a brown colour. Discard the garlic, mix together vegetables and prawns and add onions along with 8 cups of water, salt and chilli powder. Cook till the vegetables and fish is done. Add the cheese and cook for 5 more minutes. Beat the eggs in a bowl, gradually add 2 cups of hot soup stirring constantly to prevent curdling. Return to the soup in the pan. Reheat it slowly but do not allow it to boil. Place boneless pieces of fried fish in each bowl if you like before ladling in the soup.

African Peanut Soup

Ingredients (Serves 4)

- 2 cups ground roasted peanuts or groundnuts
- 4 cups each of milk or mutton or chicken stock
- 1 tblsp. cornflour
- 2 tblsp. grated onion, fried bread squares
- Grated cheese
- Salt and pepper to taste

Preparation

Mix together cornflour and milk till smooth. Mix together all the ingredients except cheese and croutons. Cook for 5 minutes. Serve hot decorated with cheese and croutons.

Australian Pumpkin Soup

Ingredients (Serves 8)

- 1/2 kilo pumpkin, peeled and cubed
- 250 grams tomatoes, peeled and diced
- 1/4 cup ground cashewnuts
- 1 big onion, mixed
- 8 cups mutton or chicken stock
- 1 tblsp. flour, 1 cup cream
- Fried bread croutons
- Salt and pepper to taste

Preparation

Fry onion till soft in 2 tblsps. of butter. Add tomatoes, pumpkin, salt, pepper and stock. Cook the pumpkin till it turns very soft. Remove from heat, cool and strain through a sieve. Mix the flour with 1/4 cup milk, add the mixture to the soup until it reaches boiling point, stirring constantly. Mix in the cashewnuts and cream. Serve with croutons.

French Onion Soup

Ingredients (Serves 6)

- 4 tblsps. butter
- 5 medium onions, minced
- 2 tblsps. flour
- 7 cups chicken or mutton stock
- 6 slices of toast
- 6 thin slices of cheese (of the toast size)
- 4 tblsps. grated cheese
- Salt and pepper to taste

Preparation

Heat butter and fry onions to a golden colour. Add into the onions, salt, pepper and flour, and stir well. Add stock gradually stirring all the time and cook the contents over a slow fire for 3 minutes. Place a slice of toast in each plate covered with the sliced cheese. Top the soup over the slices and place the plate under the grill for 1 minute, or till the cheese melts. Decorate with grated cheese, and serve.

MEAT BALL SOUP &
TOMATO SOUP

PEAS SOUP, SPINACH SOUP,
AUSTRALIAN PUMPKIN SOUP
& CHINESE EGGDROP SOUP

French Seafood Soup

Ingredients (Serves 8)

- 1/2 cup oil
- 3 medium onions, minced
- 2 flakes of garlic, 1 bay leaf
- 5 medium tomatoes, diced
- 250 grams prawns, cleaned, boiled
- 500 grams different varieties of fish, boneless
- 1 lobster, cut into small pieces, boiled
- 1 cup white wine
- 1/4 tsp. saffron dissolved in 1 tblsp. hot water
- A little grated cheese
- Salt and pepper to taste

Preparation

Heat oil and fry onions, garlic and bay leaf till soft. Add tomatoes and cook till thick. Then add all the spices, fish, 10 cups of water and wine. Cook till the fish is done. Place prawns, lobsters and fish in each plate and pour soup on top mixed with saffron. Sprinkle cheese over each plate.

RUSSIAN BORSCHT

Ingredients (Serves 6)

- 500 grams beef or mutton bones
- 2 flakes of garlic, 1 bay leaf
- 3 sprigs parsley
- 6 medium beets, 2 carrots, 2 stalks of celery
- 1/2 cup shredded cabbage
- 1 onion
- 250 grams cubed bacon
- 3 egg whites, stiffly beaten
- 4 tblsps. cream
- Salt and pepper is taste

Preparation

First prepare the stock by boiling the bones in 3 glasses of water. Before boiling place a small bag containing garlic, parsley and bay leaf in the vessel. Chop the vegetables and the bacon finely. Strain the stock and discard spice bag. Put vegetables, bacon and salt into the stock, and cook till bacon is done. Strain through fine sieve. Fold the egg whites into the soup and simmer slowly, stirring all the time. Serve with 1 tblsp. cream in each bowl.

Mexican Corn Soup

Ingredients (Serves 5)

- $2^1/_2$ cups boiled corn
- 3 medium tomatoes, peeled and pureed
- 4 cups mutton or chicken stock
- 1 cup cream
- 1 onion, finely sliced
- Salt and pepper to taste

Preparation

Put 2 cups corn along with tomatoes and a little stock into the blender and blend to a smooth puree. Heat 2 tblsps. butter and fry the onion till soft. Add into the onion, corn mixture, stock and seasonings and cook for a few more minutes. Pour the cream in and decorate with the remaining corn.

Mexican Potato and Cheese Soup

Ingredients (Serves 6)

- 2 medium potatoes, peeled and chopped
- 6 cups chicken stock
- 2 flakes of garlic, minced
- 1 medium onion, minced
- 100 grams deseeded capsicums
- 100 grams cheese
- 1 can cream-style corn
- 1 red capsicum, deseeded and cut into strips
- Salt and pepper to taste

Preparation

Cook potatoes in the stock till soft. Strain through a sieve. Heat 2 tblsps. butter and fry garlic and onion till soft. Add capsicums and seasonings into the onion and fry for a while. Add corn and cheese. Serve as soon as the cheese melts.

Chinese Fire Pot

This soup is prepared and eaten by the guests themselves.

Ingredients (Serves 12)

- Take 125 grams vermicelli
- 1 whole chicken, skinned and deboned
- 500 grams boneless lean beef
- 250 grams small prawns
- 250 grams spinach
- 250 grams each of carrots, capsicums, cucumbers, french beans and peas
- 10 cups chicken stock
- Salt and pepper to taste

For Sauce

- 8 eggs
- 1 cup soya sauce
- 1/2 cup brandy
- 4 tblsps. chilli sauce
- 1/2 cup sesame seed or til oil

Preparation

Blend all the sauce ingredients in the electric blender till smooth. Slice the chicken and beef very very thinly. Keep an electric hot plate on the dining table and put a vessel on the electric hot plate. Pour the stock in the vessel. Bring the stock to a boil and let it boil. All the meats are placed in separate bowls which are placed on the table. The food is cooked by the guests themselves by dipping the slices of meats with the help of a long fork one at a time into the simmering stock and holding it there until it is cooked to the desired degree. The cooking process is fast because the food is very thinly sliced. The cooked food is dipped into the sauce by each guest and eaten hot. The meats are eaten first. The vegetables and vermicelli are added to the stock at the end and cooked for 5 minutes and served in small bowls to the guests. At this point rice can be served if so desired.

Chinese Pork Ball Soup

Ingredients (Serves 4)

- 100 grams noodles cooked according to the directions on the noodles pack
- $2^1/_2$ cups chicken stock
- 2 green onions, chopped finely

For Balls

- 250 grams ground pork
- 2 tsps. cornflour
- 2 tsps. brandy
- 1egg white, beaten
- Salt to taste

Preparation

Mix all the ball ingredients. Make small balls and keep aside. Heat chicken stock with 2 cups of water to boiling. Add salt and put in meat balls one at a time. Cook over medium heat till the balls start floating on the top. Remove meat balls in a plate. Cook noodles in stock for 5 minutes, add the balls and cook for 5 minutes. Decorate with onions and serve at once.

Chinese Hot and Sour Pork Soup

Ingredients (Serves 5)

- 100 grams cooked boneless pork, shredded
- 5 cups chicken stock
- $1^1/_2$ cups mixed vegetables, like carrots, french beans, cucumber and cabbage
- 1/2 cup cooked ham, shredded
- 3 eggs, beaten

For Soya Sauce Mixture

- Mix together 2 tblsps cornflour mixed in 1/4 cup water
- 2 tblsps. soya sauce
- 1/2 tsp. pepper, 2 tblsps. vinegar
- 1/4 tsp. monosodium glutamate and tobasco sauce
- Salt to taste

Preparation

Bring stock to a boil. Add vegetables. When they are almost cooked, add the meats and soya sauce mixture. Stir till the soup gets thickened. Slowly pour in beaten eggs in a fine thread,stirring gently serve hot.

Chinese Mandarin Soup

Ingredients (Serves 5)

- 1 cup raw pork, cut into thin strips
- 1/4 cup sliced mushrooms
- 1/2 cup sliced carrots
- 1/2 cup sliced spinach
- 1 cup sliced celery
- 8 cups chicken stock
- 1 tsp. monosodium glutamate
- 1egg, slightly beaten
- 2 tblsps. cornflour
- Salt and pepper to taste

Preparation

Heat 4 tblsps. oil and fry the pork to red colour. Add the stock and spices and cook till the pork is almost done. Put in the vegetables and continue cooking till the pork is cooked. Mix cornflour in $^1/_2$ cup of water and add to the soup. Cook till the soup turns little thick. Mix in egg and stir quickly for 1 minute. Serve hot.

Chinese Egg Drop Soup

Ingredients (Serves 4)

- 4 cups chicken stock
- 1 medium tomato, peeled and sliced
- 4 tblsps. bamboo shoots, shredded
- 1 egg, lightly beaten
- 2 tblsps. boiled peas
- 1 tblsp. oil
- Salt and pepper to taste

Preparation

Heat the stock to boiling, then put in it tomato, salt and bamboo shoots and boil for 5 minutes. Add egg slowly stirring all the time. Top the soup with peas and oil, and serve.

Cold Soups

Chilled Tomato Soup

Ingredients (Serves 8)

- 4 medium tomatoes
- 1 bottle ketchup
- 2 medium capsicums, 2 medium cucumbers
- 1 cup good quality vinegar
- 1 flake of garlic, 1 tsp. salt
- 2 large onions
- 1 tblsp. tobasco sauce
- 1 cup each of olive oil and water

Preparation

Chop onions and garlic. Remove seeds from cucumber, capsicums and tomatoes and chop them finely. Pour vinegar, water and salt over chopped pieces, and keep aside for a few hours. Put all the vegetables, onions and garlic in the electric blender and blend at high speed till smooth. Strain the blended mixture and mix in it the ketchup, sauce and salt. Chill for 4 hours before serving.

Jellied Gazpacho

Ingredients (Serves 4)

- 1 large can tomato juice, 1 tblsp. unflavoured gelatin
- $1\frac{1}{2}$ cups water
- 2 tomatoes
- 1 small capsicum, 1 small cucumber
- 2 tblsps. each of olive oil and good quality vinegar
- Salt to taste

Preparation

Remove seeds from cucumber, capsicum and tomatoes and chop them finely. Pour oil, vinegar and salt on chopped pieces and keep them aside for a few hours. Soften gelatin in water for 5 minutes. Heat tomato juice, pour in the gelatin mixture and stir till the gelatin dissolves. Put the gelatin in a bowl and place the bowl in the freezer compartment. After 10 minutes, take out the gelatin and mix it with rest of the ingredients. Break with a fork, put in well-chilled glasses and decorate with slices of lime.

Strawberry Soup

Ingredients (Serves 4)

- 2 cups strawberries
- 9 tsps. sugar, 2 tsps. cornflour
- Juice of 1 lime
- 1 cup cream
- Few drops of red food colouring

Preparation

Roll a few strawberries in sugar and set them aside. Slice the remaining strawberries and boil in 4 cups water till soft. Strain the soup through a fine sieve. Add sugar and lime juice into the soup, and heat it till the sugar dissolves. Chill the strawberry soup and cream separately in the refrigerator for 4 hours. Serve decorated with cream and whole strawberries.

Vichyssoise Soup

Ingredients (Serves 4)

- 3 small potatoes
- 4 medium green onions
- 50 grams butter
- 1/2 cup water, 1/2 litre chicken stock
- 1/2 cup thick cream
- Salt and pepper to taste

Preparation

Use only the white part of the green onions. Thinly slice the green portion and keep it for decorating. Melt butter and cook the white part of onions till soft. Add to cooked onions, potatoes, water, stock and salt. Cook till the potatoes are soft. Mash the mixture and strain it through a sieve. Add cream. Chill. Decorate with green part of the onions.

Tomato Tea

Ingredients (Serves 4)

- 1 lime cut into thin slices
- 1 tin canned tomato juice
- 1 tin Worcestershire sauce
- 1/3 tsp. salt
- 1/4 tsp. monosodium glutamate

Preparation

Mix all the ingredients and decorate with lime slices. Chill thoroughly, and serve.

REFRIGERATOR SOUP

Ingredients (Serves 4)

- 250 grams finely sliced vegetables, like french beans, carrots and cabbage
- 50 grams very finely cubed paneer or cottage cheese. Handful of very finely sliced parsley
- 5 cups water
- 1/2 tsp. monosodium glutamate
- 1 tblsp. cornflour
- Salt and pepper to taste

Preparation

Dissolve cornflour in 1/4 cup water. Boil remaining water with monosodium glutamate. Add to it vegetables, salt, paneer and boil for 5 minutes. Then put in cornflour, slowly stirring all the lime till the soup turns a little thick. Chill and serve decorated with parsley.

Soups made with Basic Soups

Fish Soup

Ingredients (Serves 4)

- $1\frac{1}{2}$ cups basic tomato soup
- 1 onion, 1 potato
- 1 cup each of diced celery, corn kernels and flaked, cooked fish
- 50 grams grated cheese

Preparation

Heat 2 tblsps. butter and fry the onions till soft. Add potato, celery, corn and salt. Fry the mixture lightly and then add either 2 cups water or fish stock. Mix in the tomato soup and cook till the vegetables are done. Add the fish and half of the cheese. Sprinkle remaining cheese on top. Serve hot.

Vegetable Soup

Ingredients (Serves 4)

- 3 green onions, 2 medium onions
- 4 small carrots, 1 small turnip
- 4 stalks of celery
- 75 grams lean bacon, diced
- 3/4 litre basic mutton soup
- 50 grams grated cheese
- Salt and pepper to taste

Preparation

Slice onions, celery and turnips and carrots. Heat butter and fry the bacon till crisp. Add 1 tblsp. of white flour and fry for a few minutes. Add the mutton soup gradually and bring the mixture to a boil. Add vegetables and simmer till soft. Sprinkle grated cheese on top and serve hot.

Cream of Potato Soup

Ingredients (Serves 4)

- 250 grams peeled and sliced potatoes
- 1/2 litre basic mutton soup
- 1 big onion, 1 bay leaf
- 25 grams each of butter and white flour
- 2 cups milk, 1 cup cream
- Chopped parsley

Preparation

Bring the mutton soup to a boil, then add in it potatoes, onions and seasonings. Cook the mixture till it becomes soft. Discard the bay leaf and pass the mixture through a sieve. Heat butter, add flour and fry lightly, gradually add the milk stirring all the time till the soup turns smooth and thick. Add potatoes and mix in cream. Serve hot decorated with parsley.

Mixed Vegetable and Chicken Soup

Ingredients (Serves 5)

- 1 cup each of diced carrots and pumpkin
- 2 cups each of basic tomato and mutton soup
- 25 cashewnuts
- 2 tblsps. each of shredded mutton and chicken
- 1 tsp. cumin seeds
- 1/4 cup coriander leaves
- 2 cups of coconut milk
- 1 tblsp. each of flour and butter
- Salt and pepper to taste

Preparation

Grind cashewnuts, cumin seeds and coriander leaves to a paste. Heat basic soups and add vegetables and cook till vegetables become soft, strain the mixture through a sieve. Mix ground paste in 1 cup coconut milk and add to the strained soup. Heat butter, add flour and fry lightly. Add the remaining coconut milk, stirring all the time. Mix in ground paste and bring the soup to a boil. Decorate with meats. Serve hot.

Peas Soup

Ingredients (Serves 2)

- $1\frac{1}{2}$ cups shelled peas, 4 cups basic mutton stock
- 25 grams vermicelli, lightly fried
- 1 tblsp. each of butter and flour
- Fried bread croutons
- Salt and pepper to taste

Preparation

Boil peas in little water till they become very soft. Strain the peas soup through a sieve. Heat butter, add flour and fry lightly. Add the soup gradually stirring all the time till it turns a little thick. Mix in the peas and cook for a few more minutes. Then mix in vermicelli and serve immediately with bread croutons.

Carrot Soup

Ingredients (Serves 2)

- 2 cups diced carrots
- 4 cups basic tomato soups
- 4 tblsp. each of butter and flour
- 1/4 cup boiled peas, 1 small onion, minced
- Fried bread croutons
- Salt and pepper to taste

Preparation

Heat 1 tblsp. ghee and fry onion lightly. Add to the fried onions, carrots and tomato soup, and cook till carrots turn soft. Pass the soup through a sieve. Heat butter, add flour and fry lightly. Add 1/4 cup milk or water stirring all the time till the mixture becomes thick. Mix in the soup along with seasonings. Add peas and bread croutons and serve hot.

Spinach Soup

Ingredients (Serves 5)

- $1\frac{1}{2}$ cups spinach, ground to a paste
- 3 cups basic mutton soup
- $1\frac{1}{2}$ cups basic tomato soup
- 1/2 cup cream
- 1 tblsp. each of butter and flour
- 1/4 cup milk
- Fried bread croutons
- Salt and pepper to taste

Preparation

Fry the onion in ghee lightly. Add into the onions, mutton and tomato soups and spinach. Cook the mixture for 5 minutes. Heat butter, add flour and fry lightly. Add milk stirring all the time till the mixture turns thick. Then put it into the soup slowly. Pour cream on top and decorate with bread croutons.

Non-Vegetarian Soups

Fish Soup

Ingredients (Serves 4)

- 4 cups water
- 1 medium onion, finely sliced
- 3 medium tomatoes, peeled and pureed
- 1/4 tsp. each of ground cinnamon and cloves
- 2-3 sprigs coriander leaves
- 1/2 kg pomfret, cut into slices
- Salt and pepper to taste

Preparation

Cover all the above ingredients with water except spices and coriander leaves. Cook till the fish flakes easily. Lift the fish out of the broth and remove head, skin and bones. Put the fish into the broth again. Simmer for 5 minutes, sprinkle chopped coriander leaves and spices on top. Serve hot.

Fish Balls in Tomato Soup

Ingredients (Serves 5)

- 500 grams pureed tomatoes
- 1 tblsp. sugar, 1 tsp. ginger paste
- 1 tblsp. cornflour dissolved in 1/4 cup water
- 1 onion, chopped

For Balls

- 1 cup boiled and flaked fish
- 1 tblsp. cornflour, 1 tsp. ginger, minced
- 1 green onion, minced
- Salt and pepper to taste

Preparation

Mix the ball ingredients together and make small balls. Deep fry the balls to a golden colour. Cook tomatoes with ginger and onions. When soft, pass through a sieve. Add 1 glass water. Add cornflour and sugar. Again cook till thick, put fish balls in it and decorate with grated cheese as desired.

Prawn Chowder

Ingredients (Serves 5)

- 2 cups small prawns, cooked
- 2 cups cubed potatoes
- 1 cup each of thinly sliced carrots and celery
- 1 cup cream-style canned corn
- 2 cups milk
- Salt and pepper to taste

Preparation

Cook potatoes, celery and carrots in 8 cups of water. When done, add rest of the ingredients, and bring the mixture to a simmering point. Serve immediately.

CHICKEN SWEET CORN SOUP
& MUSHROOM SOUP

CARROT SOUP

BEANS SALAD & TROPICAL SALAD ▲

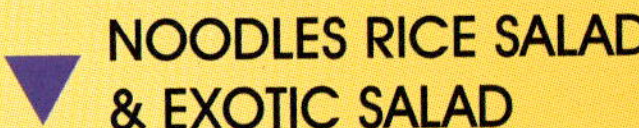

▼ NOODLES RICE SALAD & EXOTIC SALAD

Tomato and Clam Soup

Ingredients (Serves 6)

- 3 dozen clams
- 750 grams tomatoes, blanched
- 5 cups chicken stock
- 1 tblsp. sliced green onions
- $1^1/_2$ tblsps. cornflour dissolved in 1/4 cup water
- Salt and pepper to taste

Preparation

Boil clams until they open. Pick out the meat and wash the sand out. Heat 3 tblsps. oil and fry the tomatoes till soft. Mash the tomatoes to a paste and pass through a sieve. Add chicken stock, clams, pepper and salt and cook for 5 minutes. Add onions and cornflour. Stir till the soup gets slightly thickened. Sprinkle 1 tblsp. sesame seed or til oil on top.

Sweet Corn and Crab Soup

Ingredients (Serves 4)

- 1 cooked crab
- 1 tin sweet corn
- 5 cups chicken stock
- 1 tblsp. brandy, 2 eggs
- 1/4 tsp. monosodium glutamate
- 1 tblsp. cornflour dissolved in 1/4 cup water
- Salt and pepper to taste

Preparation

Bring the stock to boil. Add corn and cook for 5 minutes. Add brandy, spices, meat and cornflour. Cook till thick. Pour beaten eggs, slowly stirring all the time. Serve hot.

Sweet Corn and Chicken Soup

Ingredients (Serves 6)

- 2 cups cooked shredded chicken
- 1 tsp. brandy, 1/4 tsp. monosodium glutamate
- 2 egg whites, lightly beaten
- 1 cup noodles cooked according to the directions on the noodles pack
- 8 cups chicken stock
- 1 can cream-style sweet corn
- Salt and pepper to taste

Preparation

Bring the stock to a boil, add wine, sweet corn and eggs. Keep on stirring for 1 minute. Mix in rest of the ingredients and serve hot.

Paneer and Chicken Soup

Ingredients (Serves 5)

- 4 large tomatoes, peeled and pureed
- 50 grams each of finely sliced paneer and shredded chicken
- 1 litre chicken stock
- $1\frac{1}{2}$ tblsps. soya sauce, 1 tblsp. vinegar
- 1 tblsp. cornflour dissolved in 1/4 cup water
- 1/2 tsp. monosodium glutamate
- Salt and pepper to taste

Preparation

Put tomatoes in the chicken stock and cook for 5 minutes. Make a mixture of vinegar, soya sauce, monosodium glutamate and cornflour. Add this mixture to stock and keep stirring till the soup thickens. Add paneer and chicken. Serve hot.

Spinach and Chicken Soup

Ingredients (Serves 5)

- 500 grams spinach ground to a paste
- 1 $^1/_2$ litres mutton or chicken stock
- 125 grams shredded cooked chicken or mutton
- 1 tblsp. cornflour dissolved in 1/4 cup water
- Salt and pepper to taste

Preparation

Boil spinach in the stock for 10 minutes. Add the remaining ingredients and cook till the soup thickens. Serve hot.

Chicken and Noodle Soup

Ingredients (Serves 5)

- 100 grams egg noodles boiled according to the directions on the noodles pack
- 6 cups chicken stock
- 1/2 cup cooked and shredded chicken
- 1 cup shredded mushrooms
- 1/2 cup shredded cabbage
- Salt and pepper to taste

Preparation

Heat stock to a boil. Add the vegetables and boil the mixture for 10 minutes. Mix in rest of the ingredients and boil for 5 more minutes. Serve hot.

Chicken, Cabbage and Noodle Soup

Ingredients (Serves 4)

- 100 grams egg noodles cooked according to the directions on the noodles pack
- 5 cups chicken stock
- 2 tblsps. shredded cabbage
- 1 cup boiled and shredded chicken
- Pinch of monosodium glutamate
- Salt and pepper to taste

Preparation

Bring stock to a boil. Add cabbage and boil for 5 minutes. Mix in rest of the ingredients. Serve hot.

Chicken and Nut Soup

Ingredients (Serves 4)

- 1/4 cup each of cashewnuts and blanched almonds
- 4 cups chicken stock
- 2 tblsps. butter
- 1 cup cooked shredded chicken
- 4 cups chicken stock
- Pinch of nutmeg
- 1/4 cup brandy
- 1 onion, chopped
- Salt and pepper to taste

Preparation

Fry almonds, cashewnuts and onions to a golden colour. Grind the fried mixture to a paste with 1/2 of the chicken. Mix the remaining ingredients except brandy. Simmer for 5 minutes over low fire. Mix brandy and serve hot.

Chicken Ball Soup

Ingredients (Serves 5)

- 2 bunches of spinach
- 1 stick of celery
- 4 medium onions
- 1 tblsp. cornflour dissolved in 1/2 cup water
- 500 grams tomatoes
- 1 tblsp. ground til
- 50 grams powdered groundnuts
- Salt and pepper to taste

For Chicken Balls

- 1/2 cup shredded chicken
- 2 tblsps. cornflour, 2 green chillies, minced
- 1 egg, 1 small onion, minced
- Bread crumbs
- Handful of coriander leaves
- Salt to taste 1/4 tsp. ajinomoto or monosodium glutamate.

Preparation

Mix all the chicken ball ingredients together. Make balls and roll them in crumbs, and deep fry to a golden colour. Cook together spinach, celery, onions and cook mixture the with tomatoes in 2 glasses of water. When done, puree in a blender. Reheat soup, add til and groundnuts and cornflour. Cook the soup till it becomes thick. Pour the soup over the balls and serve hot.

Mutton Soup Deluxe

Ingredients (Serves 4)

- 500 grams mutton
- 150 grams tomatoes
- 1/2 cup gram dal
- 1 tsp. grated ginger
- 250 grams peas , boiled
- Handful coriander leaves
- 2 egg, 4 tblsps. cornflour
- Bread crumbs
- 100 grams grated cheese

Preparation

Cut the bones off the mutton and put to cook in 1 litre water along with tomatoes, gram dal and ginger. Mince mutton and mix with peas, coriander, eggs, cornflour and salt. Make ball and roll them in crumbs and deep fry to a golden colour. Strain the soup. Put the balls in soup and simmer it for 5 minutes. Serve decorated with cheese.

MEAT BALL SOUP

Ingredients (Serves 4)

- 1 cup pureed tomatoes
- 1/4 cup vinegar, 2 tblsps. sugar
- 1 tblsp. cornflour blended with 1/4 cup water
- 250 grams mixed shredded vegetables like french beans,carrots, cabbage and peas, boiled

For balls

- 200 grams minced mutton
- 1 medium potato, boiled
- 1/2 tsp. grated ginger
- 1 small onion, 1/4 tsp. monosodium glutamate
- 1 egg, 4 tblsps. cornflour
- Salt and pepper to taste

Preparation

Mix together all the ball ingredients. Form the resultant mixture into balls. Deep fry the balls to a golden colour. Mix together 2 cups of water, tomato, vinegar, sugar and salt. Cook the mixture for 15 minutes. Add cornflour and vegetables and when the soup becomes thick, put in the balls. Serve hot decorated with chopped parsley if you like.

Mutton Rivoli Soup

Ingredients (Serves 4)

- 4 cups chicken or mutton stock
- 1 cup cream
- 4 tblsps. chopped parsley

For Rivoli

- 250 grams refined flour or maida
- 2 eggs, 3 tblsps. water. salt to taste

For Tilling

- 250 grams cooked minced mutton
- 1 onion, minced, 1 tsp. chilli paste
- 1 tsp. grated ginger
- 1/4 tsp. monosodium glutamate
- 1 cup cooked spinach
- Salt and pepper to taste

Preparation

Prepare a stiff dough with flour, eggs, water and salt. Heat 2 tblsps. oil and add ginger, onion and chilli paste. Fry lightly, then add meat and spinach and cook till the mixture turns thick. Roll out the dough as thinly as possible. Cut it into squares. Put the filling in each square and fold diagonally to form a triangle; seal the edges or openings. Boil the stock, slide in the Rivoli and boil for half an hour. Add cream before serving and decorate with parsley.

Vegetable Soups

Corn and Cream Soup

Ingredients (Serves 4)

- 2 $^1/_2$ cups cooked corn kernel
- 100 grams pureed tomatoes
- 4 cups vegetable stock
- 1 cup cream
- Salt and pepper to taste

Preparation

Grind 2 cups of cooked corn. Cook corn and tomatoes in vegetable stock. Blend the mixture in the blender. Reheat the blended mixture, add spices and put in cream. Decorate with remaining corn.

Corn Soup with Vegetables

Ingredients (Serves 4)

- 1 tin creamed corn
- 6 cups of water
- 1 tblsp. monosodium glutamate
- 1$^1/_2$ tblsps. cornflour dissolved in half cup water
- 1 egg, slightly beaten
- Handful of fine noodles
- 2 tblsps. each of cabbage, carrots and french beans
- Salt and pepper to taste

Preparation

Put monosodium glutamate in water and bring to a boil. Reduce heat, put in all the vegetables and boil for 5 minutes. Add corn and boil for another 5 minutes. Then add cornflour to the soup. When the soup thickens slightly, add egg gradually, stirring all the time. Mix the boiled noodles in the soup and serve in individual bowls. This soup tastes delicious with soya and chilli sauce and vinegar chillies.

Sour Vegetable Soup

Ingredients (Serves 4)

- 200 grams mixed shredded vegetables like carrots, cabbage, french beans, peas and green onions
- 2 tblsps. soya sauce
- 2 tblsps. cornflour
- 3 tblsps. vinegar
- 1/2 tsp. monosodium glutamate
- 2 eggs, beaten
- Salt and pepper to taste

Preparation

Mix together soya sauce, cornflour, vinegar, salt, pepper and monosodium glutamate. Put 1 litre water to boil, add cornflour mixture to the water, stirring all the time till the soup turns quite thick. Add to the soup, beaten eggs slowly stirring all the time. Mix the vegetables and serve immediately.

Mix Vegetable Soup

Ingredients (Serves 4)

- 500 grams tomatoes, peeled
- 250 grams finely sliced vegetables like turnips, cabbage, french beans and peas
- 100 grams moong sprouts
- 1/2 tsp. monosodium glutamate
- 100 grams noodles boiled according to the directions on the noodles pack
- Salt and pepper to taste

Preparation

Heat 4 tblsps. oil and add tomatoes, and cook till soft and dry. Mash the cooked mixture to a paste, and put in all the vegetables , spices and cover with 5 cups of water. When vegetables are done, mix in the noodles. Serve hot decorated with green onions.

Lung Fung Soup

Ingredients (Serves 6)

- 8 cups vegetable stock
- 1/2 cup cubed carrots
- 1/4 cup sliced cauliflower
- 1/2 cup shredded french beans
- 8 mushrooms shredded
- 2 tblsps. each of soya sauce and vinegar
- 1/4 tsp. monosodium glutamate
- 1 tblsp. cornflour dissolved in 1/2 cup water
- Salt and pepper to taste

Preparation

Boil vegetables in stock. Add all the seasonings and then cornflour. Cook the soup till it thickens. Decorate with chopped green onions.

Soup with Dumplings

Ingredients (Serves 6)

- 1 large tomato
- 1 turnip
- 2 onions, 2 capsicums
- 3 carrots
- 1 stalk of celery
- 1 cup lettuce
- 1 apple, 1/4 cup parsley
- 3 tblsps. chopped dill
- Salt and pepper to taste

For Dumplings

- 1 cup refined flour or maida
- 1 tblsp. baking powder
- 100 grams curd
- 1 egg, 1 tblsp. chopped parsley
- 1 tsp. lemon juice
- Salt and milk to taste

Preparation

Boil all vegetables in 2 litres of water. Strain through a sieve. Mix all the dumpling ingredients together with enough milk to form a thick batter. Heat soup in a pan and drop batter with the help of a teaspoon. Cover and cook for $^1/_2$ an hour. Serve hot.

Cauliflower Soup

Ingredients (Serves 2)

- 1 small head cauliflower
- 1 tsp. ginger paste
- 3 cups mutton or vegetable stock
- 1 tblsp. butter and refined flour
- 1/4 cup cream
- 1 onion, grated
- Handful of chopped parsley
- Salt and pepper to taste

Preparation

Heat 1 tblsp. butter and fry onion till soft. Add to the fried onions, cauliflower, ginger and 2 cups of water. Boil for half an hour. Break fine with fork and add stock. Melt butter, add flour and fry lightly, then add soup and cook till thick. Mix in the cream and decorate with parsley.

EXOTIC SOUP

Ingredients (Serves 8)

- 1 kilo tomatoes, peeled and pureed
- 1 tsp. ginger paste
- 1 carrot, diced
- 1 bunch of spinach
- 2 hard-boiled egg yolks, minced
- 1/2 cup refined flour or maida
- 1 cup milk
- 4 tblsps. ground cashewnuts
- 1/2 tsp. grated nutmeg
- 6 tblsps. grated cheese
- 1 tblsp. sugar
- 4 tblsps. butter
- A few drops each of red, yellow and green food colouring
- Salt to taste

Preparation

Put tomatoes, ginger and carrots in a pan along with 6 cups of water. Cook till the vegetables are done. Strain the soup through a sieve. In a large pan, melt 1 tblsp. of butter, add 1 tblsp. flour and mix till smooth. Pour in the soup, gradually stirring continuously till it becomes smooth. Cook for a minute and remove from fire. Cook spinach and grind it to a paste. Melt the remaining butter and add flour, salt and nutmeg, then add milk gradually and cook till smooth. Add cheese and cook till thick.

Remove half of the mixture and set aside. In the remaining mixture, add spinach and green food colouring and keep on stirring on a slow fire till thick. In the other half of the mixture, add egg yolks and yellow colouring and also cook this till mixture thick. Place the soup on a gentle fire and add nuts, salt, sugar and red colouring. When the soup starts boiling, make small balls of the two mixtures and drop them alternatively into the soup. Let the soup boil for a couple of minutes. The soup tastes as delicious as it looks with green and yellow balls floating on red soup.

Pumpkin and Cream Soup

Ingredients (Serves 4)

- 500 grams pumpkin, chopped
- 1 large onion, chopped
- 6 cups mutton or vegetable stock
- 1 egg yolk, 1/2 cup cream
- Salt and pepper to taste

Preparation

Boil onion and pumpkin till it becomes soft. Strain the mixture through a sieve. Beat egg and cream thoroughly and beat into the soup. Mix in salt and pepper and heat thoroughly. Serve hot.

Salads

Sauces and Dressings

Sauces go very well with practically any type of salad. At the same time, they give an added flavour to any salad with which they are combined. Here are a few famous sauces and salad dressings. Use them in your salads and see how they add a zest to even your most prosaic salads.

Mayonnaise Sauce

Ingredients

- 2 tsps. french mustard
- 1 tsp. salt, 2 tsps. sugar
- 1 egg yolk
- 1/4 cup each of vinegar or lemon juice and olive oil
- 1 tsp. pepper powder
- Chilli powder to suit the taste
- 6 tblsps. cream (optional)

Preparation

Put mustard, salt, sugar, pepper, chilli powder and egg yolk in a mixing bowl. Blend all the ingredients together. Add 1 tsp. of lime juice and a few drops of oil, beating the mixture thoroughly with the help of an egg beater. Continue adding oil by drops, beating the mixture after each addition until the mixture thickens. Add the lemon juice whenever the mixture turns too stiff. Use up all the oil and lemon juice, beating the mixture continuously. Beat in the cream before serving.

Eggless Mayonnaise Sauce

Ingredients

- 5 tblsps. cream
- 2 tblsps. lime juice
- 1 tsp. each of french mustard and sugar
- 6 tblsps. olive oil
- Salt to taste

Preparation

Blend all the ingredients in a blender until the sauce reaches a smooth consistency.

Cream Salad Dressing

Ingredients

- 1 cup whipped cream
- 1 tblsp. french mustard
- 1 tsp. salt
- 2 tblsps. lemon juice

Preparation

Mix together mustard, salt and lemon juice and beat in the cream till mixture turns stiff.

French Dressing or Vinaigrette

Ingredients

- 1 cup olive oil
- 1/2 cup vinegar
- Salt and pepper to taste

Preparation

Beat together all the ingredients till they are well-mixed.

Salad Dressing

Ingredients

- 1 tsp. french mustard
- $1^1/_2$ tblsps. sugar, 1 tblsp. flour
- $1^1/_2$ tblsps. melted butter, 1/4 cup vinegar
- 1 egg, 1 cup boiling milk

Preparation

Mix dry ingredients with beaten egg. Add butter and then hot milk. Stir the mixture over boiling water till it turns thick. Remove the mixture from the boiling water and beat in it vinegar. This dressing can be kept for a month in the fridge.

How to Prepare Simple Everyday Salads

In this book I have already taught you how to make more elaborate salads. But for daily serving, you can prepare salads with minimum of ingredients in just a matter of minutes. These salads are not only appear quite appetizing, but also taste delicious. Moreover, these have minimum of calories and are health giving.

Fruit Salads

Grapefruit: Sprinkle grapefruit pulp with sugar. Chill and serve decorated with chopped glace cherries.

Grapefruit and Orange: Mix together equal quantities of grapefruit and orange pulp. Sprinkle with lime juice and sugar and serve chilled.

Watermelon: Cut out balls from watermelon pulp. Sprinkle the balls with sugar and lemon juice. Serve decorated with chopped mint.

Oranges: Orange pulp should be sprinkled with lemon juice and sugar and decorated with chopped mint pineapple and strawberries.

Mix equal amounts of diced pineapple with chopped strawberries. Sprinkle on top sugar and orange juice.

Strawberries and Cherries: Combine chopped strawberries with equal quantity of stoned cherries. Sprinkle sugar and lemon juice on top. Decorate with chopped blanched almonds.

Vegetable Salads

Beetroot: Soak thin slices of boiled beetroot and thin onion rings in salad dressing. Arrange them on dish with beetroot below and onions on top. Decorate with chopped coriander leaves and chillies.

Stuffed Beetroot: Cut small boiled beetroots into neat halves. Scoop out the centre. Stuff with chopped scooped out beetroots, tomato, cucumber, onion and moisten with salad dressing. Decorate with chopped coriander.

Celery: Mix cream cheese with mayonnaise sauce, then mix in shredded celery.

Cucumber: Slice cucumber very thinly. Set the slices aside for 15 minutes. Drain and moisten with salad dressing. Decorate with chopped coriander.

Capsicum: Cut green or red capsicums into match-stick like strips and moisten with french dressing or mayonnaise.

Potatoes: Cook potatoes. When soft, peel and cube the potatoes. Add finely sliced onion, green chillies and coriander. Moisten with mayonnaise sauce and decorate with mint.

Tomato and Capsicum: Slice tomatoes, add strips of capsicums and chopped onion. Dress with oil, vinegar and seasonings. Decorate with chopped coriander.

Cabbage and Tomato: Mix shredded cabbage with strips of capsicum and chopped onion, and tomato. Dress with oil, vinegar and seasonings and decorate with coriander.

RULES FOR PREPARING SALADS

The most important dish in a menu is the Salad. Made mostly out of raw vegetables and fruits, salads are full of nutrition and contain such essential elements of diet as vitamins A, B, C, iron, calcium, potassium, magnesium and sodium. All these nutrients are very essential for maintaining both external and internal health of the body.

Practically every vegetable that is cooked can be eaten raw especially when it is young and tender. Therefore, preparing a salad daily need not present any problem.

There is no dearth of fresh crisp vegetables like lettuce, tender spinach, tomatoes, cucumber, carrots, radishes etc. Served with an appetizing dressing, salads are fun to prepare and eat every day. Nearly all culinary herbs like parsley, celery, coriander and mint taste delicious in salads and so are fruits, fish, prawns, chicken, mutton and ham. These elaborate salads make a dish that is a meal in itself.

The important rules for making good salads are:

1. Green vegetables like lettuce, spinach etc. should be put in a salad at the last minute only, otherwise they wilt quickly. If they are limp, put them in cold water for 20 minutes only and they will turn crisp. Salad greens not required for immediate use should be stored in a polythene bag in the fridge and in a damp cloth outside fridge. They should be washed in water to which a pinch of potassium permanganate has been added to cleanse thoroughly.

Radishes: These should be washed in water and dried. The small round red ones can be served without peeling, whilst the larger ones taste better when peeled and sliced. The tender leaves can be served with the radishes.

Green Onions: Remove the outer skin of onions and its green tops, leaving a little green intact. Wash in cold water and serve either sliced or whole.

Cucumber: It should be washed, dried and eaten preferably unpeeled so that you eat all the valuable vitamins which lie in its skin.

Cabbage: Choose a firm cabbage only. Cut away the outer leaves and use only the inner leaves for a salad. Immerse the cabbage in salted cold water for 15 minutes to remove insects. Shake off surplus moisture and slice thinly or shred it.

Root Vegetables: Carrots, turnips, beetroots etc. should be grated or cut into very thin strips. They should be cut just before serving otherwise they will lose their attractive colouring and much of their vitamin content.

Vegetarian Salads

Paneer and Fruit Salad

Ingredients (Serves 2)

- 250 grams paneer, crumbled
- 50 grams each of raisins and walnuts
- 100 grams seedless grapes
- A few whole pineapple slices
- 2 tblsps. vinaigrette dressing
- Lettuce
- Tomato, carrot and capsicum strips for decoration

Preparation

Mix paneer with dressing, nuts and grapes. Place pineapple slices in lettuce, put paneer on top of pineapple slices and decorate with vegetable strips.

Waldorf Salad

Ingredients (Serves 2)

- 1 cup chopped apples
- 1/2 cup chopped celery
- 1/3 cup each of chopped walnuts and mayonnaise sauce
- 1 tblsp. lime juice

Preparation

Mix together all the above ingredients and serve.

CUCUMBER CORN MEDLEY

Ingredients (Serves 4)

- 1 cup cubed cucumber
- 1 cup boiled corn
- 1/2 cup mayonnaise sauce
- 2 tblsps. chopped coriander leaves
- 1/4 cup grated coconut
- Grind together —1/4 coconut
- 3 green chillies
- Handful of coriander leaves
- 3 flakes of garlic, 1/2 inch piece of ginger

Preparation

Mix together cucumber, corn, salt, mayonnaise and chutney. Decorate with coconut and coriander.

MIXED SALAD

Ingredients (Serves 4)

- 100 grams each of carrots, french beans, peas and noodles
- 2 pineapple slices
- 1 cup cream
- 50 grams grated coconut
- 2 tblsp. castor sugar
- 100 grams cubed paneer
- 1 tsp. mustard powder
- 1tbsp. cornflour dissolved in 1/4 cup coconut milk
- Salt to taste

Preparation

Chop french beans and carrots into long strips. Boil these strips with peas. Boil noodles according to the directions on its pack. Cook cornflour mixture till thick. Mix cream, oil, sugar, mustard and salt. Add cornflour mixture, vegetables and coconut. Put the mixture in a jelly mould and chill. Invert on a plate covered with lettuce. Decorate with pineapple and sliced cherries.

Sweet potato Salad

Ingredients (Serves 5)

- 2 cups boiled and sliced sweet potatoes
- 2 cups each grated carrots and shredded lettuce
- 1 cup cooked macaroni
- 1 cucumber, sliced
- 2 capsicums, chopped
- 1 cup mayonnaise sauce
- 1 cup cream mixed with 2 tblsps. lime juice
- 2 tomatoes, chopped

Preparations

In a glass bowl, put a layer of lettuce, potatoes, macaroni carrots and capsicums. Mix mayonnaise with cream and pour over the salad. Decorate with cucumber and tomato.

Radish Salad

Ingredients (Serves 2)

- 1 radish, 1 carrot
- 2 medium cucumbers
- 1/2 stalk of celery, 1/4 beetroot

For Sauce

- 1/4 cup vinegar

Preparation

Cut the vegetables into thin long strips. Mix together sauce ingredients and pour over the vegetables. Serve cold.

Cucumber Salad

Ingredients (Serves 2)

- 6 red radishes
- 250 grams big cucumbers; cut into 2 inch lengths
- 1 small carrot, grated
- Mix together 1 tblsp. salad oil, 2 tsps. castor sugar
- 1 tblsps. vinegar and soya sauce
- 1/8 tsp. monosodium glutamate salt to taste

Preparation

Place cucumber pieces in a salad plate. Pour over them vinegar mixture and decorate with radishes and carrots.

Spicy Cabbage Salad

Ingredients (Serves 2)

- 1 small head cabbage, finely shredded

For Sauce:

- 1 tblsp. each of soya sauce and vinegar
- 1 tblsp. til oil
- Salt and chilli powder to taste

Preparation

Heat sauce and bring it to a boil. Pour the sauce over the cabbage. Chill before serving.

Capsicum Salad

Ingredients (Serves 2)

- 3 big capsicums, seeded and thinly sliced
- 2 medium tomatoes, sliced
- 1 tblsp. each of vinegar, soya sauce or til oil
- 1/3 tsp. monosodium glutamate
- 1 tsp. sugar
- Salt to taste

Preparation

Arrange capsicums over tomatoes. Mix together rest of the ingredients and put on top. Serve chilled.

Apple and Cabbage Salad

Preparation (Serves 2)

Shred a tender cabbage. Mix with 2 to 3 tblsps. chopped celery and 2 diced apples. Mix with cream salad dressing.

Potato and Apple Salad

Preparation (Serves 2)

Mix 4 medium boiled and sliced potatoes with one sliced apple. Mix with french dressing and decorate with 1 tblsp. chopped celery.

Cucumber and Cream Salad

Preparation (Serves 4)

Take 1 cup cream, mix it with 2 tblsps. lime juice. Mix in 6 finely chopped green onions and two chopped cucumbers.

Green Peas and Egg Salad

Preparation (Serves 4)

Wash lettuce and arrange on a dish. Cut the eggs in half lengthwise. Scoop out the yolks and fill the whites with boiled green peas mixed with mayonnaise sauce. Arrange the eggs on the lettuce. Mix the yolks with a little cream cheese and enough mayonnaise sauce to bind and roll into balls. Decorate the salad with these balls.

Winter Salad

Preparation

Arrange lettuce in a salad bowl. Add alternate layers of tomato, cucumber, green onions and beetroot cut into thin slices. Decorate with chopped radishes. Serve with french dressing.

Potato Salad

Preparation

Peel and cube boiled potatoes. Mix in finely chopped green onions and vinaigrette dressing. Decorate with finely chopped parsley.

Pineapple and Tomato Salad

Preparation

Put some lettuce in a salad bowl. Cut the tomatoes into neat quarters without quite cutting through. Fill the centre with crushed pineapple blended with mayonnaise sauce, and place on the lettuce.

Vegetarian Salad Lunch

Preparation

Arrange on individual plates, grated raw carrots, beetroots, turnips, cabbage mixed with tomato strips and cucumber strips, grated cheese, minced green chillies, coriander leaves, groundnuts and walnuts. Serve with french dressing and brown bread and butter.

MOULDED SALADS

MOULDED BEET SALAD

Ingredients (Serves 6)

- 4 cups beet juice
- 2 tsps. vinegar
- 2 tblsps. each of grated onion and unflavoured gelatin
- 1 small cucumber, cut into thin rounds
- 1 orange, coloured carrot, cut into thin sticks
- 1 small raddish, diced
- 1 cup mayonnaise sauce
- Salt and sugar to taste
- Shredded carrot and cabbage for decoration
- Lettuce leaves

Preparation

Soften gelatin in 1 cup beet juice. Then melt gelatin by placing the container over fire. Cool and add the remaining juice, salt, sugar and onion. Stir till the sugar dissolves. Take a jelly mould and rinse it in cold water. Place a thin layer of gelatin mixture in the mould and holding the mould on a pan of icy water. Tilt from side to side to coat the entire surface to form a uniform layer.

Arrange the vegetables on top of this layer in any pattern of your choice, then slowly pour a second layer of gelatin which should be about 1/4 th inch in depth. Place the mould in the freezer for 30 minutes. Fill the entire mould in this manner.

But see that the gelatin has congealed on each layer before arranging vegetables on it. Each layer will take about 30 minutes to congeal. You must pour only cooled gelatin mixture over each layer, otherwise it will melt the previous layer. When the whole mould is filled, chill for an hour, or until it becomes firm. Just before serving, dip the mould in hot water for a few seconds only to loosen its sides. Unmould the salad on a bed of crisp lettuce. Decorate with grated carrot and cabbage, and serve with mayonnaise sauce.

Jellied Fish Salad

Ingredients (Serves 6)

- 500 grams any white fleshed fish, cleaned and boned but not sliced
- 3 cups boiling water
- 1/4 cup each of diced celery and onions
- 2 tblsps. unflavoured gelatin blended in half cup water
- 1 cup boiled peas
- 1 cup peeled and sliced cucumber
- 1 cup firm tomato, cut into neat cubes
- $1^1/_2$ cups mayonnaise sauce
- 1/2 cup cream ,$1^1/_2$ tblsps. lime juice
- Salt to taste

Preparation

Steam the whole fish till it becomes tender. Drain carefully. Add celery, onion, spices and salt to water and boil for 35 minutes. Strain broth from vegetables. Put gelatin mixture over direct heat and dissolve, stirring constantly. Add gelatin to the broth along with lime juice and allow the mixture to cool.

Rinse a mould with cold water and place the fish in the centre. Pour the gelatin on top. Put in the freezer compartment for $1^1/_2$ hours or till firm. Just before serving dip the mould in hot water for a few seconds only to loosen its sides. Unmould the salad on a bed of lettuce. Mix the vegetables with sauce and cream. Serve the mould surrounded by the vegetable mixture.

TOMATO RING

Ingredients (Serves 4)

- 2 cups tomato juice
- 2 cloves, 1 bay leaf
- 1 onion, 1 cup water
- 2 tsps. unflavoured gelatin
- 2 tbsps. each of sugar and lime juice
- A few drops of orange red food colouring
- 1 cup cream, salt to taste

Preparation

Soften gelatin in water. Simmer, to gather tomato juice, cloves, bay leaves and onion for 5 minutes. Strain the juice and discard the onion and spices. Add softened gelatin and sugar to the juice and cook over a slow heat till the gelatin dissolves. Cool and mix in the colour and lime juice. Pour the mixture into a ring mould rinsed in cold water. Place the mould in the freezer compartment and chill for 1/2 an hour. Just before serving, dip the mould in hot water for a few seconds only to loosen its sides. Unmould the salad on a bed of crisp lettuce. Mix the vegetables of your choice with mayonnaise sauce and cream. Fill the centre of the mould with vegetable mixture and arrange the remaining around the base of the mould.

Salad Supreme

Ingredients (Serves 6)

- 150 grams each of boiled fish chunks and prawns.
- For the first layer — 1 tblsp. gelatin
- 1/4 cup each of cold and hot milk
- 1/2 cup cream
- 1 tsp. onion juice
- Salt to taste

For Second Layer:

- $1\frac{1}{2}$ cups tomato juice
- 1 cup orange juice
- 1 tblsp. gelatin
- 1/4 cup chopped celery
- 1/4 cup boiled peas
- 1 tblsp. lime juice
- A few drops of orange and red food colouring

For Decoration:

- 1 cup mayonnaise sauce
- 2 tblsps. hot chilli sauce
- 2 cucumbers, diced into thin rings
- 2 tart apples, quartered
- Lettuce leaves

Preparation

First, to prepare the first layer, soften gelatin in cold milk, then dissolve in it hot milk. Cool it, add fish, prawns, onion juice and salt. Fold in cream. Rinse individual moulds in cold water and put in them the mixture filling till half full. Chill for half hour.

While the first layer is getting chilled, prepare the second layer as follows: Soften gelatin in orange juice. Heat tomato juice and add it to the orange juice. Mix till the gelatin dissolves. Add lime juice and colour. Cool and add celery and peas. Cool thoroughly and pour in the mould over the firm first layer. Chill again for one and half hours or till firm. Dip the mould in hot water for a few seconds to loosen its sides. Unmould the salad on lettuce and decorate with apple wedges and cucumber slices. Serve with mayonnaise sauce mixed with chilli sauce.

SUMMERTIME CHICKEN SALAD

Ingredients (Serves 6)

- 2 cups cooked and chopped chicken
- 1 cup mixed boiled vegetables like peas, carrots and french beans
- 1 tblsp. unflavoured gelatin
- 1/4 cold water
- 2 cups chicken stock
- 1/4 cup mayonnaise sauce
- Dash of pepper
- 1/2 cup minced celery
- 1/2 cup chopped capsicums
- 1 tblsp. chopped green onions

Preparation

Soften the gelatin in cold water for 5 minutes. Heat stock, mix in gelatin. Cook the mixture till gelatin dissolves. Cool and mix in mayonnaise sauce. Mix in the remaining ingredients and put in a mould which has been rinsed in cold water. Chill till the salad becomes firm. Just before serving, dip the mould in hot water for a few seconds only, and then unmould the salad on a bed or crisp greens.

JELLY SALAD &
STUFFED CUCUMBER SALAD

MUSHROOM PASTA SALAD
& EGG DRESSING SALAD

Cold Meat Mould

Ingredients (Serves 8)

- 500 grams cooked sliced mutton
- 500 grams boiled peas
- 500 grams boiled carrots
- $1\frac{1}{2}$ cups of water in which the vegetables were boiled (stock)
- 1 tblsp. brandy
- $1\frac{1}{2}$ tblsps. unflavoured gelatin
- 1 hard-boiled egg, sliced
- Mayonnaise sauce
- Salt and pepper to taste

Preparation

Sprinkle gelatin on vegetable stock for 5 minutes to soften, then heat the water till the gelatin dissolves. Rinse out a mould in cold water and pour little gelatin in it to cover the base. Hold over ice till the base firms a little.

Arrange peas in a pattern on it. Place the mould in the freezer for 5 minutes. Mix together meat, egg, half of the peas, one-third of the carrots, brandy and seasonings with the remaining gelatin. When the mixture becomes completely cool, pour it over the peas in the mould. Allow the salad to set for a few hours or till it turns firm. To serve, unmould the salad on lettuce leaves, mix the remaining vegetables with mayonnaise sauce and arrange as a garnish round the mould.

Goblet Salads

This way of serving a salad is particularly suitable for buffet as it can be eaten with a spoon or a fork.

Crab Cocktail

Ingredients (Serves 2)

- 2 cups cooked crab meat

- **For Cocktail Sauce:** 1 tblsp. mayonnaise sauce
- 3 tblsps. ketchup
- 2 tsps. lime juice
- 1/4 tsp. french mustard
- 1/4 tsp. Worcestershire sauce
- 2 drops of tobasco sauce

Preparation

Mix all the sauce ingredients in a bottle and shake well. Chill the sauce and crab meat separately and serve in lettuce-lined glasses.

Mixed Meat Salad

Ingredients (Serves 4)

- 300 grams mixed cooked meat like tongue, ham, mutton
- 2 hard-boiled eggs
- Handful of sliced parsley
- 2 green onions, sliced thinly
- 3 tblsps. olive oil, 2 boiled potatoes, peeled
- 1 tsp. french mustard
- $1\frac{1}{2}$ tblsps. lime juice
- Salt and pepper to taste

Preparation

Mix together olive oil, lime juice, mustard, salt and pepper and shake well. Cut the meat in thin match-like strips. Finely chop the potatoes and eggs. Mix with dressing and chill. Shred lettuce finely and put in the bottom of serving glasses. Put meat and egg mixture on top. Decorate with parsley and green onions.

Prawn and Grape Cocktail

Ingredients (Serves 2)

- Few lettuce leaves, shredded
- 1 tomato, cut into thin slices
- 2 tblsps. cream
- 4 tblsps. mayonnaise sauce
- 250 grams seedless grapes
- 200 grams cooked prawns
- 1 lemon cut into thick slices
- Parsley

Preparation

Put lettuce and tomato in separate cocktail glasses. Mix mayonnaise and cream and pour over half of it over the tomato. Put equal quantity of prawns and grapes in the two glasses, and top with remaining mayonnaise sauce. Decorate the top of each glass with a lemon slice and little parsley.

Seafood Salads

Seafood Salad Special

Ingredients (Serves 8)

- 500 grams prawns, shelled and cleaned
- 2 tblsps. lime juice
- 5 pepper corns
- 500 grams cooked and flaked fish
- 2 carrots, cut into match-stick like strips
- 100 grams french beans, cut into strips
- 250 grams baby potatoes, boiled and peeled
- 250 grams green peas, shelled
- 2 tblsps. minced coriander leaves
- 1 tblsp. lime juice

- **For Sauce:** 1 flake of garlic
- 1/2 cup mixed nuts of your choice
- 3 hard-boiled egg yolks
- 1 $^{1}/_{2}$ cups cream mixed with 2 tblsps. lime juice
- Salt and pepper to taste

- **For Garnishing:** 1 flake of garlic
- 1/2 cup mixed nuts of your choice
- 3 tblsps. minced parsley
- 3 hard-boiled eggs, shelled and sliced

Preparation

Boil the prawns in salted water to which lime juice and pepper corns have been added. Drain when done. Steam-cook the vegetables. Add spices, coriander leaves and lime juice. Blend all the sauce ingredients in the blender.to a smooth sauce. Mix the sauce into the seafoods. Make a mound of seafood on lettuce leaves, arrange vegetables around the seafood and decorate with parsley and eggs.

Prawn Salad

Ingredients (Serves 6)

- 3 cups cooked and diced prawns
- Lettuce leaves
- 1 cup mayonnaise sauce
- 1/2 cup cream mixed with 1 tblsp. lime juice
- 1 cup chopped celery
- 14 baby potatoes, boiled and peeled
- 1/2 cup chopped cucumber
- 3 hard-boiled eggs, chopped
- Salt and chilli powder to taste

Preparation

Line a salad bowl with lettuce leaves. Mix together rest of the ingredients and put them into the bowl. Serve chilled.

Fish Salad

Ingredients (Serves 5)

- 500 grams fish, boiled and flaked
- 4 tblsps. boiled peas
- 2 small potatoes, boiled, peeled and diced
- 1 medium tomato, sliced
- 1 cucumber, sliced
- 1 hard-boiled egg, minced
- Salt and pepper to taste

For Salad Dressing:

- 4 tblsps. salad oil
- 2 tblsps. either lime juice or vinegar
- 1 tsp. grated ginger
- 1 onion, 2 green chillies
- Herbs as preferred
- Salt and pepper to taste

Preparation

Grind ginger, chillies, onions and herbs to a paste. Mix in the paste with the rest of the salad dressings. Mix together fish, egg, boiled vegetables and salad dressing. Decorate with tomato and cucumber slices.

Fruit and Nut Salads

Christmas Eve Salad

Ingredients (Serves 8)

- 3 medium beetroots, cooked and cubed
- 3 oranges, peeled, depiped and chopped
- 2 apples, peeled and chopped
- 3 bananas, peeled and sliced
- 3 slices of fresh pineapple, cubed
- Shredded lettuce
- 1/2 cup chopped groundnuts
- Seeds from 1 pomegranate
- 1 cup mayonnaise sauce

Preparation

Mix together all the fruits in mayonnaise sauce. Line a salad bowl with lettuce. Fill the salad in the centre and decorate with groundnuts and pomegranate seeds.

Orange and Apple Salad

Ingredients (Serves 4)

- 6 oranges, peeled and chopped
- 1 apple, peeled and chopped
- Salt and chilli powder to taste

Preparation

Mix together all the ingredients and serve cold.

Stuffed Apple Salad

Ingredients (Serves 6)

- 6 medium apples
- 1 tblsp. coarsely chopped walnuts
- 1 medium banana
- 6 chopped dates
- 1 tblsp. chopped celery
- Mayonnaise sauce
- Lettuce

Preparation

Cut off 1/2 inch from stalk and top of apples. Core apples and scoop out some of the centres with a pointed knife. Mix chopped apple with fruits and celery and moisten with sauce. Fill the apples with the mixture by piling it up. Serve on shredded lettuce.

Mixed Fruit and Nut Salad

Ingredients (Serves 4)

- 1/2 cup each of chopped fresh or canned pineapple
- 1/2 cup chopped orange, skinned and seeded
- 1 cup seedless grapes
- 1 medium apple, cored and chopped
- 2 tblsps. chopped nuts of your choice
- 3 tsps. castor sugar
- 1 tblsp. lime juice
- Mayonnaise sauce
- Lettuce

Preparation

Mix fruits with nuts and sugar. Sprinkle with lime juice and moisten with mayonnaise sauce. Serve over lettuce.

Mixed Fruit Salad

Ingredients (Serves 6)

- 2 mangoes, peeled and cubed
- 1 cup each of diced pineapple and apples
- 2 bananas, cubed
- 250 grams seedless grapes
- 3 tblsps. unflavoured gelatin dissolved in 1 cup hot water
- 1/2 cup mango juice. Juice of 2 lemons
- 1 cup mayonnaise sauce, 1 cup cream
- 4 tblsps. castor sugar

Preparation

Heat gelatin, add sugar, lemon and mango juice. Remove the juice from fire, mix in it all the fruits. Put the mixture in a glass bowl and set in the freezer till firm. Whip the cream with sauce and serve with the salad.

Banana Salad

Preparation

Peel bananas and cut them into three. Then cut each piece in half lengthwise and roll the pieces in chopped roasted groundnuts. Arrange on lettuce and top with french dressing.

Date and Nut Salad

Ingredients (Serves 2)

- 25 dates, stoned
- 2 tblsps. chopped raisins
- 2 tblsps. blanched and sliced almonds and pistachios
- 100 grams cream cheese
- Lettuce

Preparation

Mix together cheese, nuts and raisins. Stuff the mixture into the dates and serve over lettuce. Top the salad with french dressing.

Nut and Cheese Salad

Preparation

Mix enough cream cheese and salad dressing together to bind the mixture. Make small balls and roll them in chopped walnuts. Serve on lettuce and decorate with tomato and cucumber and carrot strips and chopped parsley.

Pineapple Salad

Preparation

Prepare balls of cream cheese and salad dressing as described in the preceding preparation. Place pineapple rings on lettuce leaves. Place a cheese ball at the centre of each ring. Decorate with apple and banana slices and top with french dressing.

Cherry and Walnut Salad

Ingredients (Serves 4)

- 1 cup whipped cream
- 1/2 cup cherries, chopped
- 1 tblsp. lemon juice
- 2 tblsp. mayonnaise sauce
- 175 grams cream cheese
- 2 tblsps. crushed pineapple
- 1/2 cup chopped walnuts
- 3 ripe bananas cubed

Preparation

Add cheese and mayonnaise to lemon juice. Mix nicely, then add fruits and put the mixture in a salad bowl. Freeze till firm. Invert on lettuce leaves and serve with mayonnaise sauce.

Salads from around the World

Smoked Eggplant Salad (Turkey)

Ingredients (Serves 4)

- 1 big brinjal
- 2 tblsp. olive oil
- 1tblsp. lime juice
- 1 capsicum, cut into thin rings
- 1 tsp. vinegar
- 1 medium onion, minced
- 2 small tomatoes, chopped
- Salt to taste

Preparation

Hold a whole brinjal with tongs over gas flame and keep on turning while cooking. Allow the brinjal skin to turn black so as to give a smoky flavour to the salad. Skin the brinjal while still hot. Place the skinned brinjal in a bowl along with lime juice, oil, vinegar and salt. Mash with a potato masher to a smooth paste. Mould the mixture into the form of brinjal. Place on a plate and decorate with tomato, capsicums and onions.

Kidney Bean Salad (Turkey)

Ingredients (Serves 4)

- 220 grams red kidney beans or rajmah, boiled
- 2 tblsps. olive oil
- Juice of 1 lime
- 4 green onions, sliced thinly
- 1 tomato, sliced thinly
- Hard-boiled egg, quartered
- 1 tblsp. each of finely sliced parsley, mint and dill
- Salt and chilli powder to taste

Preparation

Mix together beans, salt, lime juice, oil and chilli powder. Scatter green leaves and onions over the mixture. Decorate with eggs and tomatoes.

Russian Salad

Ingredients (Serves 4)

- 250 grams peas, potatoes, french beans, carrots and cucumber
- 1 beetroot, boiled, diced
- 2 hard-boiled eggs, diced
- 1 cup mayonnaise sauce
- 1/4 cup cream
- 1 tblsp. parsley leaves, chopped
- Lettuce leaves
- 2 rings of canned pineapple, diced

Preparation

Steam-cook all the vegetables except cucumber. Dice the cooked vegetables into pieces and mix with cucumber, beets and pineapple. Mix together mayonnaise, cream and vegetables. Prepare a bed of lettuce in a wooden bowl and pile it with the prepared mixture. Serve chilled, decorated with parsley and eggs.

MIXED SALAD (CHINESE)

Ingredients (Serves 4)

- 75 grams vermicelli, boiled according to the directions on the box.
- 4 cucumbers
- 2 boiled eggs
- 1 cup each of boiled and sliced ham and chicken
- Salt to taste

For Sauce:

- 2 tblsps. soya sauce
- 2 tsps. mustard powder
- 3 tblsps. vinegar
- $1\frac{1}{2}$ tblsps. sugar
- 1 tblsp. sesame seed oil

Preparation

Mix all the sauce ingredients together. Also mix together meats, eggs and vermicelli and pour the sauce over this mixture. Mix thoroughly.

Chicken Salad (Chinese)

Ingredients (Serves 2)

- 250 grams boiled and shredded chicken
- 2 small cucumbers, sliced
- 2 tblsps. cooked and shredded mushrooms
- 1/2 tsp. ginger juice
- 1 green onion, sliced
- Salt to taste

For Sauce

- 2 tblsps. til seeds, roasted and powdered
- 1 tsp. each of sugar and chilli sauce
- 1 tblsp. soya sauce
- 2 tblsps. each of vinegar and ketchup
- 1 tblsp. sesame seed or til oil
- Salt to taste

Preparation

Mix together all the sauce ingredients. Blend the sauce with the above ingredients.

Ham and Bean Sprout Salad (Chinese)

Ingredients (Serves 4)

- 2 cups moong sprouts
- 2 eggs, beaten with 2 tblsps. milk
- 2 slices of boiled ham, cut into strips
- 4 tblsps. each of vinegar and soya sauce
- 2 tblsps. sesame or til oil
- 1/2 tsp. sugar
- Salt to taste

Preparation

Form thin omelet with eggs and cut into strips. Chill sprouts. Combine vinegar, soya sauce, sugar and oil. Heat the mixture and pour it over the sprouts. Decorate with egg strips and ham.

CURD SALAD AND
TRENDY DRESSING SALAD

CORN SALAD

VINAIGRETTE MUTTON SALAD

French Onion Salad

Ingredients (Serves 6)

- 500 grams baby onions, peeled
- 2 tblsps. vinegar
- 1 tblsp. sugar
- 1 tsp. salt, 1 bay leaf
- 2 tblsps. each of sliced parsley and tomato paste
- 2 tblsps. dry white wine
- 4 tblsps. oil

Preparation

Combine all the above ingredients together and cook the mixture over a gentle flame for 20 minutes. Chill. Insert a toothpick in each onion before serving.

Shah's Salad (Middle East)

Ingredients (Serves 6)

- 2 lamb tongues, boiled, skinned and cubed
- 1 Persian melon
- 2 cups curd
- 1 cup pineapple juice
- 1 bunch of seedless grapes
- 1 tsp. each of almond essence and honey
- 1/2 cup chopped walnuts

Preparation

Using a melon scooper, scoop out small balls. Keep the shells of melon intact. Save shells for filling and some of the melon balls for decorating. Combine rest of the ingredients, and put the mixture in melon shells and decorate with melon balls. Chill and serve.

Lobster Salad (Sweden)

Ingredients (Serves 8)

- 2 boiled lobsters, removed from shells and chopped into large pieces
- 500 grams cleaned and cooked prawns
- 2 green onions, sliced
- 3 medium tomatoes, sliced
- 1 tblsp. prepared mustard
- 1 head lettuce, shredded
- 1/4 cup vinegar
- 1/2 cup olive oil
- Salt and pepper to taste

Preparation

Mix together vinegar, mustard, oil, salt, pepper and 2 tblsps. water, mix in the vegetables and chill before serving.

Capsicum Salad (Bulgaria)

Ingredients (Serves 4)

- 4 medium capsicums
- 3 tomatoes, sliced
- 2 onions and 2 cucumbers, sliced
- 3 tblsps. vinegar
- 1/2 cup olive oil
- Salt to taste

Preparation

Hold the capsicums with the help of tongs on a gas flame. Roast till the skin turns brown. Peel off the skin and cut into thin strips. Combine together all the vegetables. Mix together vinegar, oil and salt and pour over the vegetables. Mix well all the ingredients. Chill and serve.

Mixed Salad Bowl (Britain)

Ingredients (Serves 8)

- 1 firm lettuce
- 6 small green onions, chopped
- 1 sprig mint
- 1/2 tblsp. chopped parsley
- 1/2 tblsp. olive oil
- 1 hard-boiled egg, sliced
- 2 tomatoes, sliced
- 1 cucumber, sliced
- 1 cup each of grated raw carrots and turnips
- 250 grams cooked peas, carrots and french beans
- 3/4 cup mayonnaise sauce
- 1/4 cup cream

Preparation

Mix together mayonnaise sauce and cream and boiled and grated vegetables. Put onions, mint and parsley into a salad bowl. Sprinkle with salt and pepper. Add lettuce, pour oil over the mixture and toss the salad until every leaf glistens with oil. Arrange vegetables on top and decorate with eggs, cucumber and tomatoes.

Medley Salad (Britain)

Ingredients (Serves 4)

- 1 lettuce
- 4 large tomatoes
- 250 grams diced and cooked carrots, peas, turnips and french beans
- 1/4 cup mayonnaise sauce
- Salt and pepper to taste
- 1 tblsp. each of chopped mint and parsley
- 3 green onions, chopped
- 1/4 cup extra cooked peas
- 4 hard-boiled eggs, quartered
- sliced beetroot and cucumber to garnish

Preparation

Cut 1/2- inch slice from stalk end of tomatoes, remove most of the pulp and turn them upside down to drain. Chop pulp and add it to boiled mixed vegetables, mayonnaise sauce, mint, parsley, salt and pepper. Pile into tomato cases. Toss lettuce leaves with oil and salt and pepper until all the leaves are coated with oil. Put the tomatoes on lattuce leaves. Arrange eggs around the tomatoes and decorate with beetroots, cucumber and peas.

Italian Vegetable Salad

Ingredients (Serves 4)

- 1/2 cup each of red and green capsicums, chopped
- 2 tsps. chopped parsley
- 1/2 cup chopped tomatoes
- 2 tblsps. chopped celery
- 2 green onions sliced
- 6 red radishes chopped
- 3 tblsps. vinegar
- 1/2 cup olive oil
- Salt and pepper to taste

Preparation

Combine vegetables, vinegar, salt and pepper together. Add the oil very gradually, mixing thoroughly and chill.

Tomato Salad (Spain)

Ingredients (Serves 6)

- 6 firm tomatoes
- 1 cup boiled rice
- 2 eggs, hard-boiled, chopped
- 2 green chillies, minced
- 1 tblsp. each of minced parsley and onions
- 1 flake of garlic, minced
- 1 tblsp. vinegar
- 2 tblsps. olive oil
- Salt and pepper to taste

Preparation

Cut the tomatoes in half horizontally, take out the soft pulp from inside, leaving the hard flesh intact. To make the filling, mix rest of the ingredients together along with the tomato pulp. Put the filling into the tomatoes. Chill and serve very cold.

Crab Louis (England)

Ingredients (Serves 6)

- 500 grams crab meat (cooked)
- 1/2 cup mayonnaise sauce
- 1/2 cup cream
- 4 tblsps. tomato and chilli sauce
- 1 tblsp. minced onion
- 4 cups lettuce leaves (chopped)
- 2 eggs, hard-boiled
- 4 firm medium-sized tomatoes
- Salt and pepper to taste

Preparation

To prepare a Louis dressing, mix the mayonnaise sauce, chilli sauce and onion together and chill. Arrange a bed of lettuce leaves on a plate and heap crab meat on top. Circle tomatoes and eggs around the meat and serve with the dressing.

COOKERY GLOSSARY

Foodgrains

English	Spiked millet	Barley	Jowar	Italian millet	Maize (dry)	Oatmeal	Ragi
Hindi	Bajra	Jau	Juar-janera	Kangri	Makai	Jai	Okra
Tamil	Cambu	Barli arisi	Cholam	Thenai	Muka cholam	—	Ragi
Telugu	Gantelu	Barli biyyam	Jonnalu	Korralu	Mekka jonnalu	—	Chollu
Marathi	Bajri	Juv	Jwari	Rala	Muka	—	Nachni
Bengali	Bajra	Job	Juar	Syamadhan kangni	Sukna paka bhutta	Jai	—
Gujarati	Bajri	Jau	Juar	Ral kang	Makai	—	Ragi bhav
Malayalam	Kamboo	Yavam	Cholam	Thina	Unakku cholam	Oat mavu	Moothari (korra)
Kannada	—	—	Jola	—	Vonugida musikinu	Jolu	Ragi
Kashmiri	Baajr'u	Wushku	—	Shol	Makka'y	—	—

Contd...

Foodstuff	Rice (raw)	Rice (parboiled)	Rice (white)	Rice (black)	Rice flakes	Rice (puffed)	Samai
Hindi	Arwa chawal	Usna chawal	Safed chaval	Chaval (kala)	Chowla	Murmura	Kutki, Sanwali
Tamil	Pachai arisi	Puzhungal arisi	Vellai puttu arisi	Karuppu puttu arisi	Arisi aval	Arisia pori	Samai
Telugu	Pachi biyyam	Uppudu biyyam	Thella biyyam	Nalla biyyam	Atukulu	Murmuralu	—
Marathi	Tandool	Tandool ukda	—	—	Pohe	Murmure	Sava
Bengali	Atap chowl	Siddha chowl	—	—	Chaler khood	Muri	Kangni
Gujarati	Hatna	Ukadelloo chokha	—	—	Pohva	Mumra	—
Malayalam	Pacchari	Puzhungal ari	Velutha puttari	Karutha puttari	Avil	Pori	—
Kannada	Kotnuda	Kotnuda	—	—	Avalukki	—	Puri
Kashmiri	—	—	—	—	—	—	—

Contd...

English	Semolina	Vermicelli	Wheat (whole)	Wheat flour (whole)	Wheat flour (refined)	Wheat (broken)
Hindi	Sooji	Siwain	Gehun	Atta	Maida	Daliya
Tamil	Ravai	Semiya	Godumai	Muzhu godmai ma	Maida mavu	Godhumbi ravai
Telugu	Rawa	Semiya	Godhumalu	Godhum pindi	Maidha pindi	Dinchina gadhumalu
Marathi	—	Shevaya	Gahu	Gahu kuneek	Gahu kuneek	Gavache satva
Bengali	Suji	Sewai	Gomasta	Atta	Maida	Bhanga gom
Gujarati	—	—	Ghau	Ato	—	Fadia ghaun
Malayalam	Rava	Semiya	Muzhu gothambu	Gothambu mavu	Maidu tha gothambu mavu	Gothumbu ari
Kannada	—	Shavige	Godhi	Godhi	Hittu madia	Kuttida Godhi
Kashmiri	—	Ku' nu'	—	—	—	—

VEGETABLES

English	Ash gourd	Bitter gourd	Bottle gourd	Brinjal	Broad beans	Cabbage	Capsicum
Hindi	Safed petha	Karela	Ghia	Baingan	Sem	Bandhgobi	Simla mirch
Bengali	Chal kumdo	karala	Laoo	Begoon	Sheem	Badha kopee	Lonka
Assamese	Lao bishesh	—	Jati lao	Bengena	Urahi	Bondhakobi	Kashmiri jalakai
Oriya	Pani kakkaru	—	Lau	Baigana	Shimba	Patrokobi	Simla lonka
Marathi	Kohala	Karle	Dudhi	Wangi	Ghewda	Pan kobi	Bhopli mirchi
Gujarati	Petha	Karela	Dudhi	Ringna	Papdi	Kobi	Simla marchan
Telugu	Boodie gumadi	Kakara	Sorakaya	Vankaya	Pedda chikkudu	Kosu	Pedda mirappa
Kannada	Budu gumbala	Hagalkai	Sorekai	Badanekai	Chapparadavare	Kosu	Donne menasinakai
Tamil	Pooshanikkai	Pavakkai	Suraikai	Kaththarikai	Avaraikai	Muttaikosu	Kuda milakai
Malayalam	Kumbalanga	Kaypakka	Cheraikai	Vazhutheninga	Amarakai	Muttakose	Parangi mulagu
Kashmiri	Masha'ly al	Karelu	—	Waangun	—	Bandgobhi	—

Contd...

English	Carrot	Cauliflower	Cluster beans	Colocasia	Coriander leaves	Cucumber	Curry leaves
Hindi	Gajar	Phulgobi	Guar ki phalli	Arvi	Hara Dhania	Khira	Kadi patta
Bengali	Gujar	Foolcopy	Jhar sim	—	Dhonay pata	Sasha	Curry pata
Assamese	Gajor	Phoolkobi	—	Kochu	Dhania paat	—	Narasingha paat
Oriya	Gajar	Phulakobi	—	—	Dhania patra	—	Bhrusanga patta
Marathi	Gajar	Fulkobi	Govari	Alu kanda	Kothimbir	Kakari	Kadhi patta
Gujarati	Gajar	Fool kobi	Govar	Alvi	Kothmir	Kakdi	Mitho limdo
Telugu	Gajjara	Cauliflower	Goruchikkudu kayalu	Chamadumpa	Kothimeera	Dosakaya	Karivepaku
Kannada	Gajjari	Hookosu	Gorikayi	Keshave	Kottambari soppu	Southaikayi	Karibevu
Tamil	Carrot	Koveppu	Kothavarangai	Seppann kizhangu	Koththamali ilaigal	Kakkarikkai	Kariveppilai
Malayalam	Carrot	Coliflower	Kothavara	Chembu	Kothamalli ila	Vellari	Kariveppila
Kashmiri	—	Phoolgobhi	—	—	—	Laa'r	—

Contd...

English	Drumstick	French beans	Garlic	Ginger (fresh)	Green chillies	Jackfruit	Lady's finger
Hindi	Sahjan ki phali	Pharsbeen	Lassan	Adrak	Hari mirch	Kathal	Bhindi
Bengali	Sajane dauta	French beans	Rasoon	Ada (tatka)	Kancha lonka	Echore	Dhanroce
Assamese	Sajina	Faras been	Naharoo	Ada (kesa)	Kesa jalakia	—	Bhendi
Oriya	Sajana chhuin	French beans	Rasuna	Ada (kancha)	Kancha lonka	—	Bhendi
Marathi	Shevgyachya shenga	Farasbi	Lasun	Aale	Hirvya mirchya	Kawla phanas	Bhendi
Gujarati	Saragvani shing	Fansi	Lasan	Adu	Lila marcha	Phunas	Bhinda
Telugu	Munagakayalu	French chikkudu	Vellulli	Allam (pachchi)	Pachchi mirapakayalu	Letha panasa	Bendakaaya
Kannada	Nuggekai	Avare	Bellulli	Ashi Shunti	Hasi menasinakai	Yele halasu	Bendekai
Tamil	Murungaikai	Beans	Ulli Poondu	Inji	Pachchai milagai	Pila pinchu	Vendaikai
Malayalam	Muringakkaya	Beans	Veluthulli	Inji	Pachamulagu	Idichakka	Vendakka
Kashmiri	—	—	Ruhan	—	Myool martsu waungun	—	Bindu

Contd...

English	Lettuce	Lemon	Mint leaves	Onion	Parwal	Peas	Plantain flower	Plantain green
Hindi	Salad ke patte	Nimbu	Pudina	Pyaz	Parwal	Matar	Kele ka phool	Kacha kela
Bengali	Lettuce	Lebu	Poodina pata	Pyaz	Potol	Motor	Mocha	Kancha kala
Assamese	Laipaat	Nemu	Podina	—	Patol	Motormah	—	—
Oriya	Lettuce	Lembu	Podana patra	—	Potala	Matar	—	—
Marathi	Saladchi paane	Limbu	Pudina	Kanda	—	Matar	Kel phool	Kele
Gujarati	Lettuce	Limbu	Fudino	Dungli	—	Vatana	Kelphool	Kela
Telugu	Lettuce koora	Nimma	Pudhina koora	Nirulli	—	Bathanedu	Aratipuwu	Arati kayi
Kannada	Lettuce soppu	Nimbu	Pudina sopu	Erulli	—	Betani	Balo mothu	Bala kayi
Tamil	Lettuce keerai	Elumicham pazham	Pudhinaa	Vengayam	—	Pattani	Vazhaippu	Vazhaikkai
Malayalam	Uvarcheera	Cherunaranga	Pudhinaa	Ulli	—	Pattani Payaru	Vazhappoo	Vazhakka
Kashmiri	Salaad	—	—	Gandu	—	Matar	—	—

Contd...

English	Plantain stem	Potato	Radish	Red pumpkin	Ridge gourd	Snake gourd	Sweet potato	Yam elephant
Hindi	Kele ka tana	Aloo	Muli	Sitaphal	Torai	—	Shakarkand	Zaminkand
Bengali	Thor	Aloo	Mulo	Ronga Koomra	Jhinge	Chichinga	Rangalu	Kham aloo
Assamese	—	Alu	—	Ronga lao	—	—	—	Kaath aloo
Oriya	—	Alu	—	Kakharu	—	—	—	Deshi alu
Marathi	Kelecha khunt	Batate	Mula	Lal bhopla	Dodka	Pudwal	Ratale	Suran
Gujarati	Kelanu thed	Batata	Mula	Kolu	Turai	Pandola	Sakkaria	Suran
Telugu	Arati davva	Bangaala dumpa	Mullangi	Erra gummadi	Beerakai	Potlakayi	Dumpalu	Kanda dumpa
Kannada	Dindu	Aalugadde	Mullangi	Kempu kumbala	Heeraikai	Padavalai	Genasu	Suvarnagadde
Tamil	Vazhaithandu	Urulaikizhangu	Mullangi	Parangikai	Pirrkkankai	Podalangai	Sarkarai valli kizhangu	Chenai kizhangu
Malayalam	Vazhappindi	Uralakkizhangu	Mullangi	Chuvappu mathan	Pecchinga	Padavalanga	Chakkara kizhangu	Chena
Kashmiri	—	Oloo	Muj	Paarimal	Turrelu	—	—	—

PULSES

English	Bengal gram (whole)	Bengal gram (split)	Black gram (split)	Black gram (whole)	Cornflour	Cow gram`	Green gram (whole)
Hindi	Chana	Chana dal	Urad dal	Sabat urad	Makai ka atta	Lobia (bada)	Moong
Bengali	Chola	Banglar chhola	Mashkolair dal	Mashkolai dal	Bhoottar maida	Barbati	Mug
Assamese	—	Buttor dail	Matir dail (phola)	Matir dail (gota)	Moida	—	—
Oriya	—	Buta (chhota)	Biri (phala)	Biri (gota)	Makka atta	—	—
Marathi	Hurbhura	Chana dal	Udid dal	Udid	Makyache pith	Kuleeth	Mug
Gujarati	Chana	Chana nidaal	Adad ni dal	Adad	Makai no lot	—	Mag
Telugu	Sanagalu	Senaga pappu	Mina pappu	Minu mulu	Mokkajonnalu (pindi)	Ada chandalu	Pesalu
Kannada	Kadale	Kadale bela	Uddina bela	Uddu	Musukinajolada hittu	Thadaguni	Hesaru kalu
Tamil	Muzhu kadalai	Kadalai paruppu	Ulutham paruppu	Ulundhu	Chola Maavu	Karamani	Pachai payaru
Malayalam	Kadala	Kadala parippu	Uzhunnu parrippu	Uzhunnu	Cholapodi	Payar	Cherupayaru
Kashmiri	Chanu	—	Maha	—	—	—	Muang

Contd...

English	Green gram (split)	Horse gram	Kesari dal	Kidney beans	Red gram	Red lentils	Soya bean
Hindi	Moong dal	Kulthi	Lang dal	Rajma	Arhar dal	Masoor dal	Bhat
Bengali	—	Kulthi kalai	Khesari	Barbati beej	Arhar dal	Lal masoor (bhanga)	Gari kalai
Assamese	—	—	—	Markhowa urahi	Rahor dail	Masoor dail (phola)	—
Oriya	—	—	—	Baragudi chhuin	Harada dali	Masura dali (phala)	—
Marathi	—	Kuleeth	Lakh dal	—	Tur dal	Masur dal	Soya
Gujarati	—	Kuleeth	Lakh	—	Tuver dal	Masur dal	Soya
Telugu	Pesaru pappu	Ulavalu	Lamka pappu	—	Kandi pappu	Missu pappu	—
Kannada	Hesare bele	Huruli	—	—	Togar bele	Masur bele	—
Tamil	Pasi paruppu	Kollu	Vattuparuppu	—	Thuvaram parappu	Massor paruppu	—
Malayalam	Cherupayar parippu	Muthira	—	—	Thuvara parippu	Masoor parippu	Soya bean
Kashmiri	—	—	—	—	—	Musur	—

FRUITS AND DRY FRUITS

English	Almond	Coconut	Currants	Dates	Dry plums
Hindi	Badam	Nariyal	Mungaqqa	Khajur	Alu bukhara
Bengali	Badam	Narcole	Manaca	Khejoor	Sookno kool
Assamese	Badam	Narikol	Kismis	Khejur	Sukan bogori
Oriya	Badaam	Nadia	Kala kismis	Khajura	Barakoli jateeya phala
Marathi	Badam	Naral	Manuka	Khajur	Alubhukar
Gujarati	Badam	Naliyer	Kalli draksh	Khajoor	Suka Plum
Telugu	Badam	Kobbari kaaya	Endu nalla dhraksha	Kharjoora pandu	—
Kannada	Badami	Tenginakai	Dweepa dharakshi-kappu	Kharjoora	—
Tamil	Badam/vadhumai	Thengai	Karumdhraakshai	Perichampazham	Aalpacota ular pazham
Malayalam	Badam	Nalikeram/Thenga	Karuthamurthiri	Eethapazham	—

Contd...

English	Guavas	Lemon	Orange	Raisins	Walnuts
Hindi	Amrud	Nimbu	Santra	Kishmish	Akhrot
Bengali	Payara	Lebu	Kamla lebu	Kishmish	Akhrot
Assamese	Madhurium	Nemu	Sumothira	Sukan angoor	Akhrot
Oriya	Pijuli	Lembu	Kamala	Kismis	Akhrot
Marathi	Peru	Limbu	Santre	Bedane	Akrod
Gujarati	Jamrukh	Limbu	Santara	Lal draksh	Akhrot
Telugu	Jaamapandu	Nimma	Kamala Pandu	Kismis pallu	Aakrot
Kannada	Seebe	Nimbe	Kittale	Dweepadrakshi	Acrota
Tamil	Koyyapazham	Elumicham pazham	Kichilipazham	Ular dhraakshai	Akhrot
Malayalam	Perakkai	Cherunaranga	Madhura naranga	Unakkamunthiri	Akrotandi

Dry Spices

English	Aniseed	Asafoetida	Basil leaves	Bay leaf	Caraway seeds	Cardamom (brown)	Cardamom (green)	Cinnamon
Hindi	Saunf	Hing	Tulse ke patte	Tej patta	Shahjeera	Moti elaichi	Choti elaichi	Dalchini
Bengali	Mowri	Hing	Tulsi pata	Tej pata	Sajeera	Elach (tamate)	Elach (sobooj)	Daroochini
Assamese	Guwamori	Hing	Tulosi paat	Tejpaat	Bilati jira	Ilachi (muga)	Ilachi (sevjia)	Dalcheni
Oriya	Panamahuri	Hengu	Tulasi patra	Teja patra	Sahajira	Aleicha	Gijuratie	Dalachini
Marathi	Badishep	Hing	Tulsichi paney	Tamal patra	Shahjeera	Masala welchi	Welchi (hirvi)	Dalchini
Gujarati	Variyali	Hing	Tulsina pan	Tamal patra	Jiru	Elcho	Lila alchi	Tuj
Telugu	Sopaginja	Inguva	Thulasi akulu	—	Seema sopyginjale	Yalakulu	Yala kulu (pachavi)	Dalchina chekka
Kannada	Sopubeeja	Hingu	Tulasi ele	—	Caraway beejagalre	Yalakki	Yalakki (hasuru)	Dalchini
Tamil	Perumjeerakam	Perungaayam	Thulasi	—	Karunjeerakam	Elakkai (Pazhuppu)	Elakkai (pachchai)	Lavangapattai
Malayalam	Perumjeerakam	Kaayam	Tulasi	—	Karunjeerakam	Elakkaya	Pach Elakkaya	Karuvapatta
Kashmiri	—	Yangu	—	—	—	Aal budu'a aal	—	—

Contd...

English	Cloves	Coriander seeds	Cumin seeds	Fenugreek seeds	Mace	Mustard seeds	Nutmeg	Parsley
Hindi	Laung	Sukha dhania	Jeera	Methi dana	Javitri	Rai	Jaiphal	Ajmooda ka patta
Bengali	Labango	Dhonay	Jeera	Methi	Jaeetri	Sarsay	Jaifall	Parsley
Assamese	Long	Dhania guti	Gota jeera	Paleng	Janee	Sarioh guti	Jaaiphal	Sugandhi lota
Oriya	Labanga	Dhania	Jira	Methi	Jayatree	Sorisha	Jaiphala	Balabalua shaga
Marathi	Lavanga	Dhane	Jire	Methi dane	Jaypatri	Mohari	Jayphal	Ajmoda
Gujarati	Laving	Dhana	Jeeru	Methi	Jaypatra	Rai	Jaypal	Ajmo
Telugu	Lavangalu	Dhaniyalu	Jeelakara	Menthulu	Japathri	Aavaalu	Jaikaaya	Kothimeerajati koora
Kannada	Lavanga	Kottambari beeja	Jeerige	Menthe	Japatri	Sasive kalu	Jaika	Kottambari jotiya soppu
Tamil	Kraambu	Koththamali virai	Jeerakam	Vendhayam	Jaadipathri	Kadugu	Jaadhikai	Kothamalu ilaigal pole
Malayalam	Karayaamboovu	Kothamalli	Jeerakam	Uluva	Jathipathri	Kadugu	Jathikka	Malliela pole
Kashmiri	Ru'ang	Daaniwal	Zyur	—	Jalwatur	—	Zaaphal	

Contd...

English	Peppercorns	Pomegranate seeds	Poppy seeds	Red Chillies	Tamarind	Turmeric	Vinegar	Thymol
Hindi	Kali mirch ke daane	Anardana	Khus khus	Lal mirch	Imli	Haldi	Sirka	Ajwain
Bengali	Marich	Dareem bij	Posto	Paka lonka	Tentool	Halood	Seerka	—
Assamese	Jaluk	Dalim guti	—	Sukan jalakia	Teteli	Halodhi	Sirika	—
Oriya	Golamaricha	Dalimba manji	—	Nali lankamaricha	Tentuli	Haladi	Vinegar	—
Marathi	Kale Miri	Dalimbache dane	Khas khas	Lal mirchya	Chincha	Halad	Sirka	Onva
Gujarati	Mari	Dadamna bee	Khaskhas	Lal marcha	Amli	Haldar	Sirko	—
Telugu	Miriyaalu	Daanimma ginjalu	Gasagasaalu	Erra mirapa kayalu	Chinthapandu	Pasupu	—	—
Kannada	Menasina kalu	Dalimbo beeja	Gasagase beeja	Kempu menasinakai	Hunase hannu	Arasina	—	—
Tamil	Milagu	Maadhulai vidhai	Kasakasaa	Milagai vatal	Puli	Manjal	Pulikaadi	—
Malayalam	Kurumulagu	Madhala naranga kuru	Kaskas	Chuvanna Mulagu	Puli	Manjal	Vinagiri	—

Modern Cookery Book

—Asha Rani Vohra

A must for every housewife

Praises are showered on a gourmet who can churn out good dishes as well as present them well on the table.

The modern housewife is a very conscious lady and wants to move with the times. She wants to do her work better with the help of scientific equipments, technological ways and means, and give her work an artistic touch, thus saving her labour and time.

This book attempts to cater to not only the metropolitan housewives but also the small-town housewives. In order to acquaint them about how to organise parties, the etiquettes to be observed and the presentation of the food are all given for the benefit of the readers.

Apart from culinary delights from across the world, the book includes sections on:

- Ideal kitchen
- Art of serving and table decoration
- Table manners

Big Size • Pages: 144 (Also available in Hindi)
Price: Rs. 80/- • Postage: Rs. 15/-

Rapidex Courses

Adopted by CRORES of readers

The largest selling sensation of all times

A course of just 60 days can make you speak English fluently and effortlessly, whatever be your mother tongue.

Published in sixteen languages

Hindi, Malayalam, Tamil, Telugu, Kannada, Marathi, Gujarati, Bangla, Oriya, Urdu, Assamese, Punjabi, Nepalese, Persian, Arabic and Sinhalese

180/- each

All books with CD
** without CD

1201S .... Hindi	1226S .... Assamese	1210S .... Malayalam	1228S .... Nepali
1202S .... Gujarati	1211S .... Oriya	1209S .... Tamil	1130B .... Singhalese**
1207S .... Marathi	1203S .... Punjabi	1204S .... Telugu	1131C .... Persian**
1208S .... Bangla	1205S .... Kannada	1206S .... Urdu	1127A .... Arabic**

Rapidex Dictionary of Spoken Words

98/- each

6611 G .... Eng.–Hindi
1133 A .... Eng.–Bangla
1132 D .... Eng.–Tamil
1134 B .... Eng.–Kannada
1136 D .... Eng.–Telugu
1137 A .... Eng.–Gujarati
1135 C .... Eng.–Malayalam

POPULAR SCIENCE

Set Code: 4505 S

Set Code: 4510 S

• Four Volumes • Over 800 Pages
• Over 900 Illustrations • 890 Articles
Available in Hindi & English both

2214 S
Rs. 135/- (Colour)

2213 S •
Rs. 135/- (Colour)

6678 D • Rs. 180/-

6679 A • Rs. 150/-

9412 C • Rs. 96/-

A 12-Volume series teaching 6 Regional Languages through Hindi & vice versa

132/- each

1236 A .... Malayalam-Arabic

1218S .... Hindi-Bangla	1214S .... Hindi-Malayalam
1224S .... Bangla-Hindi	1220S .... Malayalam-Hindi
1219S .... Hindi-Gujarati	1215S .... Hindi-Tamil
1225S .... Gujarati-Hindi	1221S .... Tamil-Hindi
1216S .... Hindi-Kannada	1217S .... Hindi-Telugu
1222S .... Kannada-Hindi	1223S .... Telugu-Hindi

PERSONS & PERSONALITIES

2113 D • Rs. 150/-

5178 E • Rs. 72/-

8991 D • Rs. 120/-

5122 L • Rs. 72/-

51102 • Rs. 72/-

4176 B • Rs. 395/- (H.B.)

1112S ....

1234S ....

PERSONALITY DEVELOPMENT

Available in Tamil also.

9450 B • Rs. 195/- | 5642 A • Rs. 150/- | 9447 C • Rs. 88/- 8966 E • Rs. 88/- | 9973 E • Rs. 110/- | 5639 B • Rs. 80/- | 9070 B • Rs. 175/-

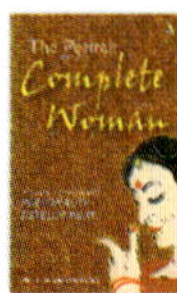

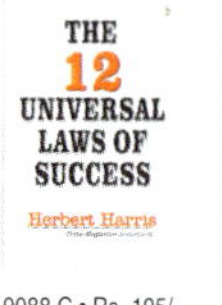

8868 D • Rs. 120/- | 9028 D • Rs. 120/- | 9981 B • Rs. 96/- | 9088 C • Rs. 195/- | 8997 B • Rs. 96/- | 9430 B • Rs.150/-

STUDENT DEVELOPMENT

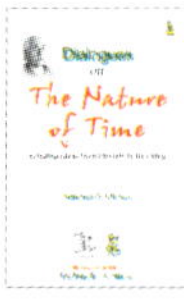

9457 E • Rs. 150/- | 9455 C • Rs. 150/- | 8962 A • Rs. 96/- | 4016 D • Rs. 96/- | 9089 D • Rs. 135/- | 9967 C • Rs. 120/-

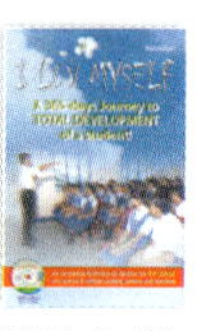

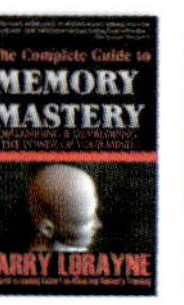

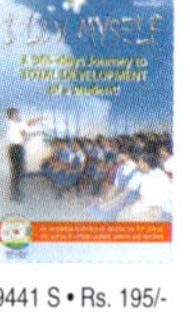

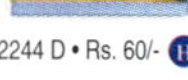
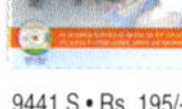

9071 D • Rs. 96/- | 2244 D • Rs. 60/- H | 9441 S • Rs. 195/- | 5622 A • Rs. 108/- | 9090 A • Rs. 160/- | 2241 J • Rs. 80/-

COMPUTERS

9471 C • Rs. 96/- | 9460 J • Rs. 120

9462 M • Rs. 150/- | 7766 A • Rs. 120/-

7712 K • Rs. 96/- | 7711 J • Rs. 96/-

PARENTING

9594 K • Rs. 80/- | 8919 D • Rs. 96/- | 8261 D • Rs. 150

BODY/BEAUTY CARE

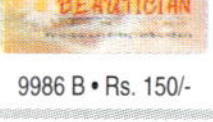

8093 D • Rs. 150/- | 9986 B • Rs. 150/- | 9922 F • Rs. 120/- | 8865 F • Rs. 90/- | 8971 B • Rs. 96/-

LOVE, SEX & ROMANCE

8260 D • Rs. 96/- | 8266 D • Rs. 80/- | 8278 C • Rs. 80/- | 8916 D • Rs. 120/- | 8268 C • Rs. 175/-

SAYINGS/QUOTATIONS/PROVERBS

8999 D • Rs. 80/- | 9953 A • Rs. 68/- | 5512 A • Rs. 120/

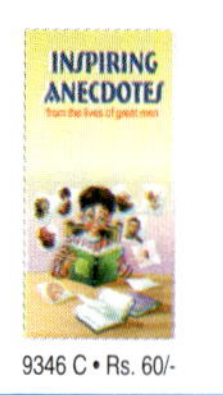

8963 B • Rs. 80/- | 9346 C • Rs. 60/- | 9425 A • Rs. 60

SELF-IMPROVEMENT

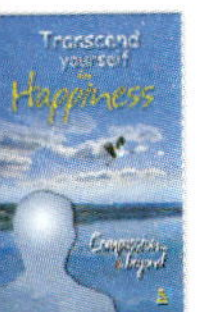

9464 R • Rs. 80/-

9096 B • Rs. 96/-

4008 J • Rs. 96/- Ⓑ

9027 D • Rs. 120-

8258 D • Rs. 120/-

9026 D • Rs. 175/-

9563 N • Rs. 125/-

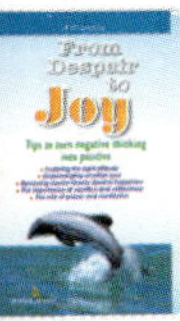

8928 D • Rs. 80/-

9066 B • Rs. 96/-

9081 D • Rs. 96/-

4010 L • Rs. 60/-

9091 B • Rs. 80/-

8885 D • Rs. 68/-

8947 E • Rs. 80/-

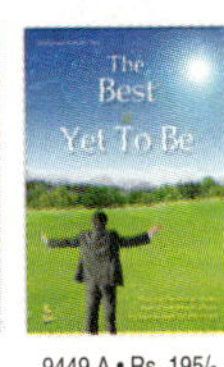

9449 A • Rs. 195/-

9466 T • Rs. 96/-

4009 K • Rs. 96/-

8943 C • Rs. 195/-

8935 D • Rs. 96/-

8990 C • Rs. 96/-

JOB / CAREER

5623 B • Rs. 195/-

9404 D • Rs. 195/-

9439 C • Rs. 150/-

9431 C • Rs.175/-

4017 D • Rs. 120/-

4018 D • Rs. 80/-

9535 C • Rs. 150/-

DIET & NUTRITION

9941 D • Rs. 96/-

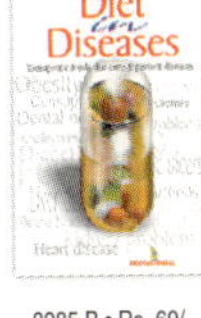

8985 B • Rs. 69/-

8904 D • Rs. 96/-

8276 A • Rs. 96/-

8968 G • Rs. 96/-

RELATIONSHIP

9458 G • Rs. 72/-

8998 C • Rs. 120/-

9438 B • Rs.150/-

9065 A • Rs. 80/-

9994 E • Rs. 120/-

ALTERNATIVE THERAPIES

8983 E • Rs. 80/-

8941 A • Rs. 80/-

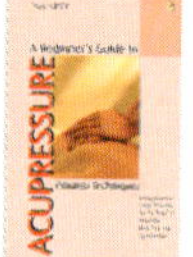

8879 C • Rs. 60/-

5637 D • Rs. 96/-

8882 F • Rs. 150/-

8842 D • Rs. 100/-

8889 D • Rs. 80/-

8836 D • Rs. 135/-

8271 C • Rs. 96/-

2317 E • Rs. 60/-

9935 F • Rs. 120/-

9950 B • Rs. 120/-

GENERAL HEALTH

8877 A • Rs. 120/-

8870 D • Rs. 60/-

9029 D • Rs. 68/-

9075 C • Rs. 160/-

9940 D • Rs. 120/-

8938 D • Rs. 88/-

8948 A • Rs. 96/-

9025 D • Rs. 80/-

9038 D • Rs. 68/-

8859 G • Rs. 80/-

SLIMMING & FITNESS

9445 A • Rs. 150/-

8277 B • Rs. 80/-

8875 K • Rs. 80/-

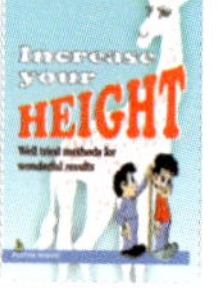

8847 M • Rs. 60/-

COMMON AILMENTS & DISEASES

8281 A • Rs. 80/-

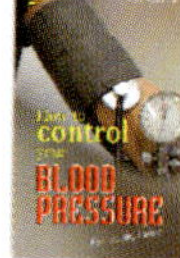

8094 D • Rs. 120/-

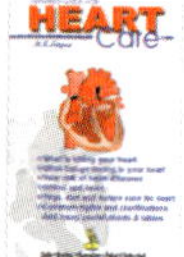

8888 D • Rs. 80/-

8908 D • Rs. 120/

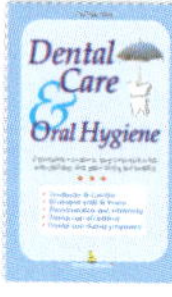

8964 C • Rs. 96/-

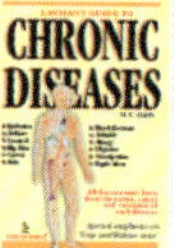

8848 D • Rs. 96/-

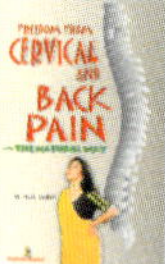

8878 B • Rs. 80/-

8891 D • Rs. 150/-

YOGA & MEDITATION

2118 F • Rs.120/-

8269 A • Rs.150/-

9087 B • Rs.120/-

9998 D • Rs.120/-

9080 C • Rs.24/-

8939 D • Rs.96/-

8099 D • Rs.80/-

8867 D • Rs.120/-

8901 D • Rs.120/-

9958 S • Rs.160/- (with CD)

2119 G • Rs.96/-

8892 D • Rs.120/-

9057 B • Rs. 96/-

HOMEOPATHY

9446 B • Rs.150/-

8887 D • Rs.175/-

8270 B • Rs.165/-

HINDOOLOGY / RELIGION

Coffee Table Books

9453 A • Rs.340/- HB

4128 D • Rs. 250/- Colour (H.B.)

4177 C • Rs. 295/- (H.B.)

9987 E • Rs. 150/-

9585 A • Rs. 96/-

9983 D • Rs. 499/- Colour (H.B.)

9508 D • Rs.95/-

4126 B • Rs. 96/-

9505 A • Rs.195/-

4183 A • Rs. 350/- (H.B.)

9514 B • Rs.60/-

4151 A • Rs. 399/- Colour (H.B.)

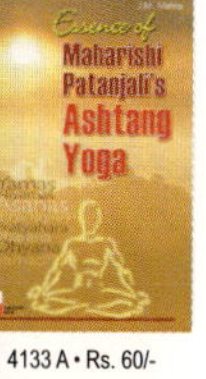
4133 A • Rs. 60/-

8898 D • Rs. 80/-

4124 A • Rs. 80/-

9405 A • Rs. 195/-

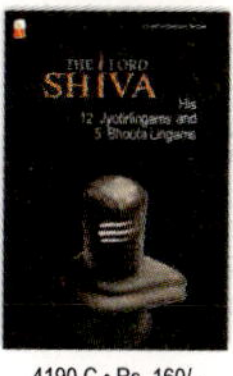
4190 C • Rs. 160/-

9984 E • Rs. 399/- Colour (H.B.)

9513 A • Rs.175/-

9520 D • Rs. 120/-

9510 B • Rs.120/-

9542 B • Rs. 150/-

4182 D • Rs. 96/-

4130 B • Rs. 120/-

4152 B • Rs. 96/-

4134 B • Rs. 80/-

9509 A • Rs.150/-

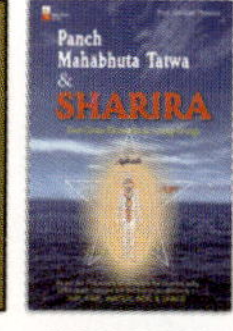
9407 C • Rs. 195/-

9525 A • Rs. 150/-

9504 D • Rs.96/-

9989 D • Rs. 96/-

4181 C • Rs. 195/-

9540 D • Rs. 150/-

9069 A • Rs. 80/-

4179 A • Rs. 295/- (H.B.)

4132 D • Rs. 80/-

9063 D • Rs. 80/-

9997 C • Rs. 80/-

Commenteries on BHAGAVAD GITA

9959 D • Rs. 80/- 4113 D • Rs. 48/- 4188 A • Rs. 160/-

COOKERY BOOKS

9936 D • Rs. 120/- 9320 A • Rs. 125/- 9297 C • Rs. 125/- 9948 D • Rs. 80/- 9962 C • Rs. 125/-

9938 D • Rs. 100/- 9942 D • Rs. 80/- 9944 D • Rs. 80/- 9943 D • Rs. 80/-

HOMEMAKING / GRILLS & RAILINGS

3111 E • Rs. 175/- 3107 F • Rs. 88/- 3106 E • Rs. 88/- 3108 G • Rs. 90/-

3102 K • Rs. 195/- (H.B.) 3103 L • Rs. 88/- 3104 M • Rs. 88/- 3105 D • Rs. 88/-

MYSTERIES / GHOSTS / ADVENTURE

2331 C • Rs. 60/- 9463 P • Rs. 100/- 9985 A • Rs. 80/- 9465 S • Rs. 100/- 9472 D • Rs. 10

5164 E • Rs. 100/- 9977 B • Rs. 96/- 2337 C • Rs. 96/- 2336 B • Rs. 80/- 51107 • Rs.100

5156 D • Rs. 72/- 5172 F • Rs. 72/- 5121 K • Rs. 72/- 5116 D • Rs. 72/- 2335 A • Rs. 8

JOKES

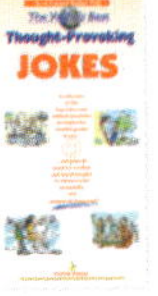

2319 B • Rs. 96/- 2341 B • Rs. 60/- 2318 A • Rs. 80/- 2330 B • Rs. 80/- 9226 A • Rs. 6

HUMOUR & SATIRE

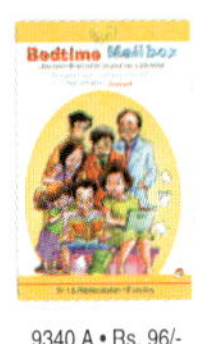

2338 D • Rs. 120/- 8890 D • Rs. 68/- 9340 A • Rs. 96/- 8927 D • Rs. 68/- 2326 E • Rs. 120/-

QUIZ BOOKS

8965 D • Rs. 96/- 7727 L • Rs. 80/- 7723 F • Rs. 72/- 7726 K • Rs. 72/- 7753 G • Rs. 72/- 7722 E • Rs. 72/- 7725 J • Rs. 72/-

Moral, Wisdom & Fairy Tales

8967 F • Rs. 80/- 9077 E • Rs. 120/-

9248 C • Rs. 60/- 2289 D • Rs. 72/-

ASTROLOGY / VASTU / HYPNOTISM / PALMISTRY

8925 D • Rs. 80/-

8899 D • Rs. 110/-

9432 D • Rs.150/-

8259 D • Rs. 88/-

2125 D • Rs. 80/-

2133 B • Rs. 96/-

2109 F • Rs. 120/-

8902 D • Rs. 80/-

2132 A • Rs. 150/-

2127 D • Rs. 150/-

9086 A • Rs. 295/- (H.B.)

2112 D • Rs. 80/-

2108 E • Rs. 80/-

2116 D • Rs. 110/-

3110 D • Rs. 96/-

2120 D • Rs. 96/-

ENGLISH IMPROVEMENT

9448 D • Rs. 175/-

5511 E • Rs. 72/-

6651 E • Rs. 175/-

5538 D • Rs. 80/-

6607 L • Rs. 88/-

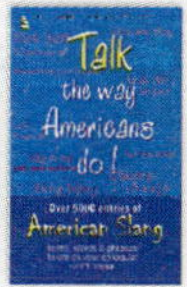

5541 C • Rs. 196/-

9040 D • Rs. 60/-

9056 A • Rs. 96/-

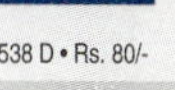

GENERAL

4022 D • Rs. 80/-HB

9041 A • Rs.195/-

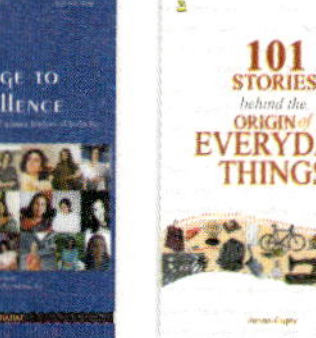

5114 B • Rs.68/-

4175 A • Rs. 195/-

9532 D • Rs. 250/- HB

MAGIC

2250 A • Rs. 110/-

2202 E • Rs. 80/-

2237 M • Rs. 60/-

2242 K • Rs. 60/-

2208 M • Rs. 80/-

2243 L • Rs. 60/-

FUN, FACTS

9470 B • Rs. 100/-

9326 B • Rs. 96/-

6690 D • Rs. 60/-

2328 G • Rs. 50/-

2275 D • Rs. 80/-

2247 F • Rs. 60/-

2327 F • Rs. 50/-

2211 F • Rs. 60/-

5110 A • Rs. 80/-

MANAGEMENT / BUSINESS & PROFESSION / STOCK MARKET

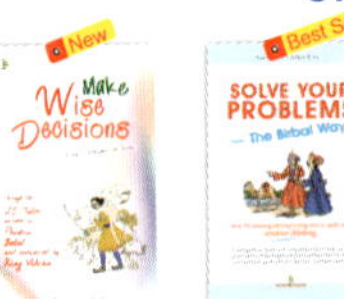

9461 K • Rs. 135/- | 5638 A • Rs. 110/- | 8979 A • Rs. 96/- | 9406 B • Rs. 150/-

5646 A • Rs. 225/- | 5643 B • Rs. 120/- | 8972 C • Rs. 80/- | 9402 B • Rs. 195/-

5614 E • Rs. 150/- | 9079 B • Rs. 195/- | 9403 C • Rs. 195/- | 5618 D • Rs. 88/-

5615 D • Rs. 150/- | 4001 A • Rs. 150/- | 4004 D • Rs. 88/- | 5641 D • Rs. 195/- (H.B.)

5640 C • Rs. 120/- | 9313 D • Rs. 150/- | 8883 D • Rs. 120/- | 4005 E • Rs. 96/-

AYURVEDA

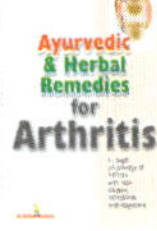

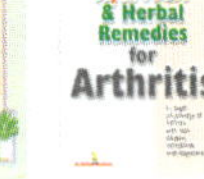

8923 D • Rs. 150/- | 8010 D • Rs. 88/- | 8944 D • Rs. 175/- | 9094 E • Rs. 96/-

FICTION from Cedar books

9459 H • Rs. 1000/- | 9583 U • Rs. 175/- | 9526 B • Rs. 125/- | 9532 D • Rs. 250/- HB

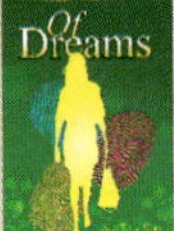
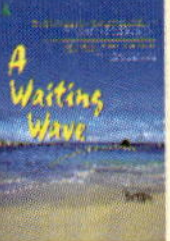

9590 F • Rs. 125/- | 9595 M • Rs. 150/- | 9801 A • Rs. 125/- | 9580 R • Rs. 175/-

9591 G • Rs. 125/- | 9588 D • Rs. 125/- | 9589 E • Rs. 150/- | 9581 S • Rs. 150/-

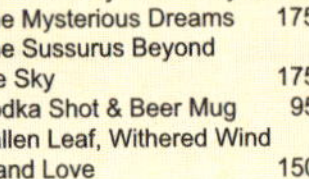

- God moved your Cheese 125.00
- Love@facebook 150.00
- Gaban 150.00
- Godaan 250.00
- What nobody ever told you 125.00
- The Mysterious Dreams 175.00
- The Sussurus Beyond the Sky 175.00
- Vodka Shot & Beer Mug 95.00
- Fallen Leaf, Withered Wind ...and Love 150.00
- Rosha 175.00
- Fate, Fraud & A Friday Wedding 150.00
- The Ultimate Laugh 150.00
- Cricket Till I Die! 150.00
- Delayed Monsoon 150.00
- What Happened to That Love 125.00
- Did you see The Joker? 125.00
- Luv U Mate 125.00
- Kalika–The Calyx 175.00
- Love was never Mine 150.00
- The K-Word 150.00
- Temple of Destiny 175.00
- The Adventure of the Bubblegum Boy 150.00
- Truly, Madly, Deeply 175.00
- The Long Road 150.00
- The Unheards 150.00
- To catch a Butterfly 95.00
- It can't be you... 175.00
- Far From Normal 150.00
- Somewhere@nowhere 150.00
- Deceivers 150.00
- Some of the Whole 199.00

- Love on Velocity Express 125.00
- A River on fire 95.00
- A Nameless Place 125.00
- Incredible High 175.00
- One Day 125.00
- Fallen Leaf, Withered Wind 150.00
- Footprints in The Bajra 175.00
- Haunting Silhouettes 175.00
- How I got my Girl Back 150.00
- Interpretation 125.00
- The Red Corridor 150.00
- The God who failed! 95.00
- Prisoners of Hate 195.00
- The Wheel Turned 175.00
- Beyond Diamond Rings 175.00
- Mask in the Mirror 295.00
- Dance O' Peacock 175.00
- Enemy in the Ranks 195.00
- Friendship@ facebook.com 175.00
- Vinculum 95.00
- Dancing on the notes of life 195.00
- Illusions of Love 195.00
- Kite Strings 175.00
- Knots and No Crosses 175.00
- Men as they are! 125.00
- Not for $ Anymore 150.00
- Three Shades of Green 195.00
- The Angel of God 195.00
- The Journey of Om 175.00
- The Second Hand 175.00
- Under the rain tree 95.00